SOCIAL MEDIA 4EVR:

Identifying, Achieving & Nurturing Social Capital

MICHAEL A. BROWN SR., PH.D.

and

TRACY SCHARIO, APR

Cover Layout by Nick Webb

ISBN: 1-4928589-1-9
ISBN-13: 978-1-4928589-1-1

Printed in the United States of America
First Printing, 2014

Right Fit Communications LLC
5007C Victory Blvd #194
Yorktown, VA 23693

www.socialmedia4evr.com

10 9 8 7 6 5 4 3 2 1

This book is dedicated to all my family and friends who put up with me throughout this journey.

- Michael

Dedicated to my family, friends and PR colleagues who give me energy and support. Thank you.

- Tracy

Welcome!

When people talk about social media, they refer to the different tools or platforms one uses to communicate socially. Social networking activities use those tools or platforms, social media, to share experiences, get advice, make decisions, develop trust, and reduce risk. So social networking is about our actions and social media is about the tools we use to energize those actions.

Social Media 4EVR is a significant change to the way people experience social media and social networking. We focus on the "why" of social media participation, allowing the destination, not the path or platform, to be the focus of your activities. This approach allows people and organizations to leverage time and efforts to promote positive social and environmental change.

The real challenge is moving your frame of reference from solely which platform to use – Facebook, LinkedIn, Twitter, etc. – to a view of goal achievement and audience targeting.

Contents

Preface

The social media journey offered in this text is about social capital – identifying it, achieving it, and nurturing it. The key to success in social media lies in managing two-way expectations, values and returns on investment of time and contributions.

Social Media 4EVR was developed as an introduction to social media and Web 2.0 and its contribution to public administration; developing an understanding of practical applications, developing knowledge of the history of digital/electronic media, and interacting with others in social media to build community. This approach presents planning practices that address goals, establish roles, and seek feedback and verification that the social media approach is working. Social media presents a fresh approach of Web-based applications and channels that offer citizens opportunities to share constructive ideas and opinions and to play active roles throughout the public sector. The processes presented herein are also called social networking, which is sometimes used interchangeably with social media. Organizations and individuals use social media to actively listen to and constantly monitor the digital conversation to learn about services, develop initiatives, and establish relationships.

This book offers new initiatives and thought processes in social media by stressing the reasons for participation, the importance of building social capital, the value propositions so important to drive networking success, and the need for planning. Overall, Social Media 4EVR has several objectives. First, readers will be able to identify social media participation expectations, value and return on investment of time. Second, readers will develop or improve their organizational or personal brand using tools and techniques provided herein. Third, readers will learn how to develop a social media plan that addresses the goals required by their organizational or personal brand.

Introduction

How about taking a journey with us? How about adjusting your social networking thought processes in a way that allows you to take advantage of one or more of the four pillars of social media strategy – communication, collaboration, education and entertainment? If you come along, there's an opportunity for you to reap the benefits of social media planning that leads to your success in conquering keys to social media participation: Expectation, Value and Return, or EVR.

∞

EVR: Expectation, Value and Return

You can achieve and/or sustain social networking success by delivering on an EXPECTATION of shared VALUE and a worthy RETURN on each participant's investment of time and attention.

Expectation, Value and Return, or EVR, is about using three keys to develop a winning social media plan that focuses your participation and encourages others to join your network. Keeping your profile alive as part of the digital conversation may prove helpful in ways you may not anticipate.

EVR is the key to social networking participation. This is how you demonstrate the WIIFM – what's in it for me – to your intended audience, whether they are one person or a group. In the truest sense of social networking, people are motivated to contribute valuable information to a person or a group. We're talking about three things. First is the ability to get useful help in a two-way arrangement, which leads to a second thing, the opportunity for a valued information exchange. The third benefit to EVR is getting and giving recognition that matters to others.

We'll cover EVR in detail in Chapter 7.

∞

The Social Media 4EVR process is based on solid strategy, valuable engagements, and effective interactions that lead to social capital. The strategy is based on one or more of Safko's (2012) four pillars of social media strategy: communicate, collaborate, educate and entertain. Valuable engagements build on content, define your brand, and establish your reputation. Effective interactions are the ways you create social capital, or value. Finally, you can sustain your success by delivering on a need to create and exchange social capital.

Because the process starts with sound strategy – a great plan – it's critical to choose the best pillar for your situation. In choosing, always analyze your audience to find out how they communicate, who they interact with, and what they need. This last thing, need, is tough, but you can figure it out if you participate in their community of interest before you decide on a pillar. Then you can think about how your intended value proposition and interaction will be perceived by your target audience.

In selecting communication or collaboration, how does your audience get their information, and with whom do they exchange? If you use education, what learning styles or academic pursuits characterize your audience? And if entertainment is your choice, it might be helpful to focus on a venue, such as Facebook friends, YouTube, Google+, etc. The key here is to determine where your target audience is posting, texting, watching videos, sharing photos, etc.

Now you can adjust your strategy to trigger the most beneficial action, response or behavior from your audience. In short, we see communication and collaboration as methods that ensure an open door for continuous interactions whenever and wherever they are available. Education is all about leveraging all of the learning styles and venues available through academic pursuits. Finally, entertainment is a way to use humor, emotion, empathy, sympathy, etc., to deliver a message and facilitate communication.

In addressing the "why" of social media, find real value that transcends time, giving you continuity. This social media journey is about social capital – identifying it, achieving it, and nurturing it. Social capital is the value or reward needed to address expectation, value and return.

Planning

Let's not forget planning as we move through this adventure. Planning is the key to success in your social networking efforts, whether personal or business related. Planning helps you achieve open communication that is vital to information discovery and delivery. Unfettered communication is the way you discuss ideas, publish news, ask questions and share links. We want to use social media to expand our audience, "recruit" people who are like-minded, and create or enlarge our reputation. The give and take can be very beneficial.

Certainly, there can be negatives to these interactions. Every day, we read about fraudulent interactions, spam and virus attacks, and identity theft, which can be a complex problem. Negative comments about our public persona or about the information we post present a threat that many want to avoid at all costs. But a plan can help you work through all of these instances. A plan is like your car insurance policy. Every day when you leave your home in your car, you know there are real threats of car accidents. But you work very hard to avoid those threats and, if something happens, you have insurance. A social media plan is like having insurance, because it contains information about privacy settings and other protections that can help.

In short, if you fail to plan, you plan to fail. As we address the "why" of social media, the plan can serve one of two purposes. If you have a plan before you engage in social media activities, it can protect you from the threats mentioned above. If you're already engaged, a good social media plan can help you make course corrections and improvements that will make your networking activities even more rewarding.

You're Not Alone

You're not alone. Every day, people around the globe try to make sense of social networking. They ask themselves any number of questions. Should I get involved? Should I be doing more? Am I using the right platform? Who should I be communicating with? This book can help with the answers, but not before creating an understanding of social networking goals, roles and interactions, and not without finding a personal plan of action.

Networking success lies in having practical applications and partnering in building community. This book addresses goals, establishes roles, and seeks feedback and verification about the approach. Table 1 provides an overview.

∞

4 Pillars and their meaning

Table 1

Communication	<ul><li>EXPECTATION: 2-way, unfettered communication</li><li>VALUE: Receive information that satisfies a need</li><li>RETURN: Create an "open door" for information</li></ul>
Collaboration	<ul><li>EXPECTATION: 2-way, unfettered collaboration</li><li>VALUE: Receive collaboration that satisfies a need</li><li>RETURN: Create an "open door" for collaboration</li></ul>
Education	<ul><li>EXPECTATION: Educate someone or some community of interest</li><li>VALUE: Satisfy a need for information that is more difficult or time-consuming to get elsewhere</li><li>RETURN: Leverage different learning styles and venues</li></ul>
Entertainment	<ul><li>EXPECTATION: Make my day better, or less bad, with what you're offering</li><li>VALUE: Ease my mind</li><li>RETURN: Create an "open door" for me to "entertain you back"</li></ul>

∞

Social Media and Social Networking

Social media presents a fresh approach of Web-based applications and channels that offer citizens opportunities to share constructive ideas and opinions and to play active roles throughout the private and public sectors. For instance, government organizations and elected officials at different levels use social media to deliver messages to citizens and create interactions in the interest of feedback and follow up. These organizations should then partner with citizens to monitor their existing services and develop new initiatives.

Let's take a moment to examine social media versus social networking to help you with terminology. When we talk about social media, we refer to the different tools or platforms one uses to communicate socially. Social networking activities employ those tools or platforms, social media, to share experiences, get advice, make decisions, develop trust, and reduce risk. So social networking is about our actions and social media is about the tools we use to energize those actions.

Let's take a closer look at social media. It is the channels we use to facilitate unfettered communication. It is characterized by the digital content and interactions by and between people that allow us to be social. Social media is any online platform or channel delivering user-generated content.

Lon Safko says simply, "social media is the media we use to be social. That's it (2012)." Safko goes on to list 15 social media categories: social networking, publishing, photo sharing, audio, video, microblogging, live casting, virtual worlds, gaming, productivity applications, RSS, aggregators, search engines, mobile and interpersonal (2012).

Social Media 4EVR does not attempt to cover all of these areas; however, two are most important: social networking and microblogging.

Social networking is about expanding social and/or business contacts by making connections through individuals. This networking, friend-of-a-friend invitation approach establishes interconnected Internet communities, or personal networks, formed to assist people in making contacts that would be good for them to know. In many cases, these are connections that they probably would not have had a chance to meet otherwise.

"Microblogging is no more than text messaging on steroids," according to Safko (2012). Examples are Yammer for behind-the-firewall communication or Twitter for open text communication. And there are of course the myriad of blogs by companies and private citizens bringing you all the latest information and tips on any subject imaginable. A blog is a website with regular entries of commentary or news. Blogs serve to establish a person or company as experts who are transparent, relevant and active. They are intended to spark conversation or create new or stronger connections.

Social Media 4EVR employs social networking to offer information, techniques and examples in several areas of discovery. First, it's important to establish and articulate the "why" of social networking participation. Along the way, you'll come to understand the social media membership lifecycle. People move through various roles over time: Visitor, Lurker, Novice, Insider, Leader and Elder. You'll learn about these and other social media terms, because knowing the "language" of the social media system is very important to your participation.

Dynamic Conversation

So, social networking is an online conversation that is not controlled nor is it organized in traditional ways. It is organic and complex. It gives individuals ways to connect and share content with friends and/or like-minded people. For businesses, it offers insight into what people say about the brand, product or service, provides a way to participate in those free-flowing conversations, and shares new ideas which may lead to better business decisions.

The ability to define and control a brand is shifting – from business to individuals. Social Media 4EVR offers ways to take advantage of that shift.

There is an increasing amount of information in the literature on social networking (Cerulo 1990, Zack and McKenney 1995, Fowler, Lawrence et al. 2004, Chung, Hossain et al. 2007), trust (Newell and Swan 2000, Nyhan 2000), measuring performance or productivity (Davis and Luthans 1980, Bearman, Guynup et al. 1985, Otis 2007, Akdere and Roberts 2008), capacity or skill building (Shetzer 1993, Segrest, Domke-Damonte et al. 1998, Eastin and LaRose 2000, Erickson and Jacoby 2003) and other constructs. However, much of the social networking literature is primarily descriptive and categorizing without providing value-creation and value-capturing strategies. This text works to make sense of the value potential available to individuals through social media and, in turn, social networking.

Social networking participation may be influenced when people are presented with evidence of a return on the investment of their time. Even if there is simply a perception of benefit, users may be more inclined to participate, or they may be moved to increase their participation levels. This value-based examination is what powers our approach to social networking and individual planning.

Social networking, then, is the umbrella term that refers to sharing and discussing information, and then energizes social media, which are primarily Internet- and mobile-based tools.

Social media sites are web-based services that allow individuals to use a protected system to construct a public or semi-public profile, maintain a list of people with whom they share a connection, and build and share their list of connections through interactive activities. The explosion of new network connections in the workplace suggests the need for an exploration of the various ways organizations can affect and improve performance and productivity or, at least, ways that workers can get better help in their social networking endeavors.

After learning some great information and techniques throughout this book, you will have a chance to hone your skills using a plan. A personal plan starts with establishing and/or revising your online presence, or brand. People who get the most out of social networking tend to use more than one social media platform, because each has its own focus and characteristics. A social media plan guides participation and allows participants to assess the effectiveness of their activities. All of these skills can be developed using the information contained in this book.

Social Media 4EVR examines social networking in a variety of ways. One way is an analysis of ways to adjust one's networking thought processes. This is done by taking a non-traditional approach to social media registration. Instead of focusing on getting started and moving right to learning the "how" of different applications and tools, Social Media 4EVR recommends you search for the "why" of networking participation. Why are you getting involved, what do you intend to accomplish, and what will be your measuring stick for when you've achieved your goals?

Along the way, we also address building or improving your brand, whether it's a personal or corporate approach. Designing a social media plan is a great way to have a roadmap for success. So, this text is about accepting the communication challenge offered in the social media world. We begin with a short history of social media, because you can't get where you're going unless you know where you've been.

Throughout this journey, Social Media 4EVR maintains a focus on keys to success in networking engagements, social capital and the 4 pillars of social media, allowing readers to determine which approach works best for their interests. We introduce EVR – Expectation, Value and Return – which is the key to social networking. Readers can compare and contrast personal and corporate branding, analyze a brand and examine current online activities.

My colleague Tracy Schario offers planning and policy implementations so critical to guiding your path, keeping your personal information safe, and ensuring there are no policy violations. This will arm readers with valuable information about designing a plan, complete with an explanation of fundamentals required, a plan template and sample plans to energize your personal social networking journey.

Social Media 4EVR is an action plan for social networking success, effectively engaging people by taking into account both personal and corporate branding considerations. The learning adventure starts with a historical perspective that addresses the theoretical evolution of social networking. We then move to an analysis of the growth and maturity of social media in general, providing tools and techniques to build social capital and engage audiences.

Engagement relies on understanding the 4 pillars of social media and using them appropriately to engage communities of interest and present the answers to the WIIFM, or "What's In It For Me?" You will find ways to build your personal brand or to understand and adapt to your corporate brand.

You will learn about brand analysis and use those results in networking activities. This approach, EVR, is all about your participation as it relates to participation of those you encounter on the social media highway or the digital conversation.

Social Media 4EVR also offers information on planning, policy, crisis communications, and on how to design a social media plan. This book is an open invitation to accept the communication challenge via social networking.

We offer some concrete objectives to help you work with us on this social networking journey on the next page. It is our sincere hope that this is a worthwhile journey for you. Let's get started.

Social Media 4EVR Objectives

1. History
   a. Identify terminology of the social media "system."
   b. Identify historical milestones in social media evolution.
2. Theory
   a. Identify theories relevant to social media success.
3. Engagement
   a. Identify the "why" of social media participation, focusing on creating social capital and an engagement strategy.
   b. Evaluate and/or revise online presence.
   c. Communicate on one or more social media platforms.
4. Four Pillars
   a. Define the four pillars of social media.
5. Building Your Brand
   a. Develop branding strategies both corporate and personal.
   b. Develop or improve your personal brand.
6. Brand Analysis
   a. Conduct brand analysis.
7. Expectation, Value and Return (EVR)
   a. Identify participation expectations, value and return (EVR).
   b. Identify the various roles in social media participation.
   c. Evaluate participation in social media.
8. Planning and Policy
   a. Develop a social media plan that addresses your goals.
9. Social Media Plan
   a. Assess social networking effectiveness based on a plan.
10. Crisis Communication
    a. Assess the effectiveness of social media in crisis situations.
11. Accept the Challenge
    a. Improve your social media participation.

Chapter 1: A Little History

CHAPTER CHALLENGE

Evaluate The Past

Philosopher George Santayana said, "Those who cannot remember the past are condemned to repeat it." And Aristotle said, "If you would understand anything, observe its beginning and its development." Some might even say that anything that happened before will eventually happen again. Regardless of which statement works for you, this chapter is about surveying the past to provide suggestions about the future. Social media is a dynamic evolution of the way people create, share and exchange information. This history is being written at warp speed, but there are some consistent threads. For instance, when people communicate they try to communicate with those who have like interests and values. They try to create social connections through their communications. Also, the need for instantaneous communication is ever present, and people always seek cutting-edge approaches and viral pursuits. To achieve social media success, we must identify the terminology of the "system." We must also identify relevant historical milestones in the evolution of social media.

Social media has shifted the way people read and disseminate information, using many-to-many models to energize and speed up communications at all levels. Even one-on-one conversations can take on a new energy through social media. This medium focuses on humanizing and personalizing stories specifically for the people we want to reach, allowing us to share information and build strong relationships. How did social media grow?

The historical review that follows focuses on adoption of innovation, which addresses decision processes that occur at the individual level. It also focuses on how users are attracted to a system and how their behavior is affected. Literature on the following are relevant for our historical review:

- Innovation adoption (2007);
- The technology acceptance model (Davis 1989, Kwon and Wen 2010);
- Governing by network (Goldsmith and Eggers 2004);
- Social capital theory (Putnam 1993);
- Social network analysis (Hatala 2006); and
- Trust.

Innovation Adoption

A key feature of this definition is that it considers that the perception of newness matters, even if absolute newness does not apply (Damanpour and Gopalakrishnan 1998, Lyytinen and Rose 2003). Innovation adoption is a way to change the interaction; a way for the individual to help with adapting to changing environments and, hopefully, to sustain or increase individual performance or at least the perception of improvement potential (Damanpour and Evan 1984, Makkonen 2008, Damanpour, Walker et al. 2009).

Innovation adoption, or connectivity, is based on the ability to become connected at a level where performance is seen as optimal and leadership has created an atmosphere capable of maintaining the necessary structural support mechanisms for information sharing and knowledge management (Hatala and Lutta 2009).

Diffusion of innovation is the process through which some innovation is communicated within a social system (Perry 2006). Perry's innovation-decision process has three main components: the innovation-decision process, the characteristics of an innovation, and adopter characteristics.

Adopter characteristics are used in social media to identify those individuals with whom one would most likely communicate.

Social media success is based on, and can be traced back to, the management of risk and uncertainty. Those are key considerations when people or organizations make participation decisions. They gravitate to people and organizations they know and trust, and often who have themselves been successful in social media activities. This lends credibility to everyone's participation. People seek credible reassurances that their attempts won't result in embarrassment, humiliation, financial loss or wasted time. People and organizations tend to see high risks in change, so they require validation from trusted peers to get a sense that they can handle the innovation or social media activity. People will also seek validation that participation will provide concrete benefits.

Technology Acceptance Model

Davis (1986, 1989) developed the technology acceptance model (TAM) that is now the most widely applied model of user acceptance and usage. TAM was adapted from the theory of reasoned action (Fishbein and Ajzen 1975, Ajzen and Fishbein 1980). Davis found perceived usefulness and perceived ease of use to be especially important determinants of system use. For perceived usefulness, he argued that people are inclined to use or not use an application to the extent they believe it will help them perform their job better. Perceived ease of use, in turn, is based on the knowledge that even if potential users believe that a given application is useful, they may, at the same time, believe that the system is too hard to use and that the performance benefits of usage are outweighed by the effort of using the application. Therefore, according to Davis (1986), system usage is theorized to be influenced by perceived ease of use.

What this means for our social media examination is that online behavior is determined by a person's attitude toward the activity and by the perception of the usefulness of the activity. It's about a reasonable return on the investment of time and attention. TAM says that even if someone doesn't welcome the interaction, they may get involved if they perceive that it will bring them some benefit in terms of improved performance, connections, income, or some other interest. The correlation between perceived ease of use and perceived usefulness is generally believed to be that if all things are equal, a person will use the process that is easiest to use.

Further, if the process is easy to use, the participant will then feel a sense of control over the activity. That sense of control motivates the activity because less effort and time are required and "spare" efforts or time can be used on other tasks.

Governing by Network

As organizations become more reliant on networks, social media tools are increasingly provided to improve business processes, create new business and enhance the lives of employees. Organizations commit to allowing employees to spend an unspecified number of hours making connections and joining communities. In *Governing by Network*, Goldsmith and Eggers (2004) provide a lens organizations can use to view and analyze social networking activities. Greater reliance on networks requires that organizations deal with making the interactions administratively effective and professionally accountable. *Governing by Network* (Goldsmith and Eggers 2004) is focused on government and its networking challenges, but the arguments presented are relevant to this examination of social networking and the individual's perception of improvement based on the activity.

The challenge for government is, in part, to rely more on a web of partnerships and alliances to meet its goals. That reliance is precisely the challenge organizations face when embarking, or continuing, on a social networking journey. Now, leaders want to know whether they can be sure their investment will lead to improvements in efficiency or performance. More important, leaders want to know why some employees reject the opportunity to participate in social networking.

The "governing by network" methods by which organizations seek administratively and professionally accountable social interactions are relevant for this social media journey (Goldsmith and Eggers 2004). The networking challenges presented and the way organizations address them are the key to ensuring a web of partnerships and alliances that foster goal achievement and personal enrichment. The views expressed may help those in leadership positions gain more insight into whether they can ensure that investments in social media activities will lead to improvements in efficiency or performance.

Governing by network is one way to promote desired behaviors that may improve performance through social networking, but it is not the only way. Social capital theory (Putnam 1993) and social network analysis (Hatala

2006) are relevant for demonstrating and taking advantage of social networking benefits.

Organizations need concrete incentives to affect employees' decisions to participate in organizational social networking activities (Hatala 2006). Related to this notion is organizational climate, which refers to the current perceptions of people in a work environment concerning the observable (social, political and physical) nature of the personal relationships that affect work accomplishment within an organization. Transfer climate is a subset of the perceptions of organizational climate concerning the transfer of training.

Organizational and transfer climates deal with perceptions, which have unique properties that influence individual motivation and behavior toward the transfer of training. An individual's perceptions of supervisor support, opportunity to use new training, level of peer support, supervisor sanctions, and positive or negative personal outcomes resulting from application of training on the job are all part of the transfer climate (Hatala and Fleming 2007). Transfer climate is relevant because social media continues to grow. Individuals want to participate in an environment that interests them and that connects them with those who share those interests. While the training aspect of transfer climate are not our primary focus, training can be very helpful in affecting desired behaviors as they relate to social networking. Because of the voluntary and generally positive participative nature of social networking, utilization of a model similar to that used in corporate training is more comfortable for the participant. The key is to facilitate participation because use of social media can reinforce positive and self-selected learned behaviors.

Social Capital Theory

Social capital theory suggests that the efficiency of society can be improved by facilitating coordinated actions. For organizations, social networking is a two-step, voluntary process where one accepts or rejects participation. It should be possible to develop a framework that identifies participation determinants and opportunities. Effective social networking requires creating networks that feature fluid communications and benefits that are easily understood. Social networking may be beneficial for companies dedicated to understanding the challenge of achieving desired behaviors (Putnam 1993).

Social networking is similar to social capital theory in that it represents resources that are embedded in a positive social structure (which reinforces norms and values). Norms and values are easily accessed and or mobilized in purposive actions by the participant. Bolino et al (2002) defines social capital as a resource derived from relationships among individuals, organizations, communities, or societies, and argues that these resources are reflected by the existence of close interpersonal relationships among individuals. Social networking has the same characteristics; however, there is quite often no face-to-face communication and the relationships can often be much more informal than those characteristic of social capital-building activities. Social capital practices are often meant to build relational contracts between and among employers, employees and coworkers within an organization (Leana and Buren 1999).

Social Network Analysis

Social network analysis offers ways to understand how relationships are structured. Social networks are made up of individuals or organizations that we refer to as "nodes." Nodes are tied to or connected by one or more specific types of interdependency, such as common interest, kinship, friendship, financial exchange, sexual relationships, dislike, or relationships of beliefs, knowledge or prestige. In the interest of social media, we examine network ties, or the relationships between the actors, so that we can understand the structure among actors, groups and organizations. We also explain the variations in beliefs, behaviors and outcomes.

It is important to examine organizational climate and transfer climate, which highlight the need for concrete incentives to convince employees to participate (Hatala 2006). Organizational climate focuses on current perceptions of people in a work environment and their observable personal relationships that affect their performance (Hatala and Fleming 2007).

Transfer climate is a subset of the perceptions of organizational climate concerning the transfer of training. These constructs are beneficial because they shed light on an individual's perceptions of supervisor support, opportunity to use new training, level of peer support, supervisor sanctions, and positive or negative personal outcomes resulting from application of training on the job (Hatala and Fleming 2007).

Trust

Trust has a relationship to dependence, satisfaction and commitment. Trusting relationships in organizations involves an ongoing decision to give most people the benefit of the doubt, and it can be extended even to people one does not know from direct experience.

Examining trust as it relates to social media participation and community interactions requires an examination of two central issues. The first involves trust as a means for dealing with uncertainty. The second focuses on trust and acceptance of vulnerability (Newell and Swan 2000). Luhman (1988) argues that trust occurs in situations of risk and uncertainty:

"A system requires trust as an input condition in order to stimulate supportive activities in situations of uncertainty or risk."

Luhmann's notion suggests that trust is an attitudinal mechanism that allows individuals to subjectively assess whether or not to expose themselves to situations where there may not be an acceptable trade-off in terms of possible damage versus received advantage. The attitude develops when individuals have accepted vulnerability to others.

Social Media 4EVR focuses on several aspects of trust which can be used to shed light on social media participation. The trust relationship where expectation, leadership, organizational culture and technology are involved is relevant. Expectation involves the value that each individual expects to receive from personal or organizational interactions. Leadership involves how leaders can influence the trusting relationship with employees, and how employees want and expect trusting interactions to be created and maintained.

Organizational culture involves whether the culture adequately connects to employee values, norms and beliefs in a way that is enduring and productive. Finally, technology involves the level of confidence individuals have that the technology is something that they can effectively use, and whether they can truly benefit from participating in that use.

From innovation adoption to technology acceptance to governing by network to social capital theory to social network analysis to trust, we have discovered the foundations of the social media environment we live in.

Social media provides a vital source of information and numerous opportunities for all participants to build social capital. Researchers Igbaria and Tan (1997) suggest that investigations into information technology applications should focus on the impacts of accepting or rejecting such tools and capabilities. If employees perceive that there is some return on the investment of their time or attention in terms of improved skills or the availability of new challenges or increased standing in the firm, they may be more inclined to participate in the organization's social media tool of choice.

A good social media plan helps individuals make the personal decision to participate with four focus areas.

- Adjusting social networking thought processes;
- Personal branding that promotes personal or organizational goals and objectives;
- Designing a personal social media plan; and
- Accepting the challenge and adventure of unfettered communication that is social networking.

Chapter 2: Social Media Theory

═══════════════════ ∞ ═══════════════════

Theory

This chapter identifies theories relevant to social networking participation and success. A theoretical examination helps us understand how perception can influence engagements. In general, theory is a systematic way of understanding events, behaviors and situations. For the purposes of this journey, we are most interested in human and organizational behavior. Theory gives us a set of interrelated concepts, definitions and propositions that explains or predicts events or situations by looking into relationships and the way they are intertwined. Theories are important to give us a starting point for an examination, and they help us find answers to questions we have that have already been answered. For instance, when we focus on human behavior and why people trust or do not trust, we can rely on relevant theories like innovation adoption or various theories on trust. Social networking activities can be enhanced by identifying theories relevant to participation and success.

═══════════════════ ∞ ═══════════════════

Social networking and its "digital conversations" continue all day every day whether we are listening or not. At this point, it is important to provide some theoretical background on social networking and its importance to online exchange of information. Successful exploration of new social media opportunities can be enhanced through a theoretical examination.

There are several theories that are relevant for individuals and organizations alike, and most are suggested by the short history we provided in the previous chapter. The theories include innovation adoption, governing by network, trust, social capital, social learning, social network analysis, and the Hawthorne effect.

These theories are based on how positive perceptions can have a significant impact on participation. In fact, there are a number of studies on innovation adoption (Hatala and Fleming 2007), governing by network (Goldsmith and Eggers 2004), social capital theory (Putnam 1993), and trust (Grey and Garsten 2001). Let's start with innovation adoption theory, which evaluates internal decision processes, attraction to a networking system, and behavioral implications. Knowledge of social networking adoption behavior provides vital information and opportunities to grow personal and professional networks. It's important to focus on adoption and diffusion, which refer to the ability to manipulate the social networking behavior of others, or to a person's ability to manage their online behaviors in a constructive way. Innovation adoption, or connectivity, is based on the ability to become connected at a level where performance is seen as optimal and where there is an atmosphere capable of maintaining the necessary structural support mechanisms for information sharing and, for organizations, knowledge management (Hatala and Lutta 2009).

Diffusion of innovation is the process through which some innovation is communicated within a social system (Perry 2006). Perry's innovation-decision offers important insights into the process of social change, which we can apply to social networking. Diffusion of innovations demonstrate what qualities make an innovation spread successfully. The theory also focuses on the importance of peer-to-peer conversations and networks, and on understanding the needs of different user segments.

Network Governance

Social networking insight can also be gained by examining the governing by network theory (Goldsmith and Eggers 2004), which involves helping organizational participants ensure that network-based partnerships are administratively effective and politically accountable. On an individual basis, it's important to create partnerships that can be effectively managed based on time spent and attention required, and that feature accountability on the part of all parties involved. In the case of government, officials should move away from having employees view themselves as doers and instead try to create a culture where employees view themselves as facilitators, conveners, and brokers of how to engage the community's talents to accomplish the task at hand. All of the groups mentioned above can benefit from a web of partnerships, contracts and alliances to create and enhance participation in social media activities.

Network initiatives can therefore help in accomplishing objectives with measurable performance goals, assigned responsibilities to each partner, and structured information flow. The ultimate goal of these efforts is to produce the greatest possible value proposition, greater than the total of what each participant could accomplish on his or her own without collaboration (Goldsmith and Eggers 2004).

Effective network governance that enhances performance first requires people who can do several things, like master the challenges of goal alignment, provide oversight, avoid any communications meltdown, and coordinate multiple players. It's also important that people manage the tension between competition and collaboration, and overcome data deficits and capacity shortages. The actions mentioned above can be personal and/or professional considerations.

The next consideration under governing by network is more organizational than personal, and it is about addressing issues of mission and strategy.

Leaders can assist with individual performance improvement by starting with mission and then determining the process; a much-needed change from the tradition of deciding on a process and then trying to fit it to a mission. This allows the destination, not the path, to be the focus around which the components and interactions of the network are built (Goldsmith and Eggers 2004). It's also important to address what members of the network ought to do. Ask the right question in terms of what outcome-based value proposition, or public value, the organization is trying to create. Once those decisions are made, it important to communicate those intentions to employees.

Leaders must always pay attention to cultural compatibility when selecting network partners. This is essential for fostering long-standing, mutually beneficial relationships. The key is shared values across the culture. Creating ties that bind is related to cultural compatibility, and it requires that effective network ventures establish dependable communication channels, coordinate activities between network participants, and build trusting relationships. The challenge, however, goes beyond simply using the technology to manage relationships. Social networking still requires vigilance in addressing people issues, examining processes, aligning values, and building trust. Finally, network integrators must create and maintain the infrastructure and conditions that support long-term relationship building. Network governance, knowledge sharing, value and incentive alignment, trust building, and overcoming cultural differences are challenges every good integrator must face head on.

When responsibilities are managed effectively, they can open the door to the enormous value available to participants, whether they are from business, from government, or from an individual's home. The value is available because of the varied and unlimited points of contact that can be translated into useful responses by those involved in the network, allowing each to adjust their responses appropriately. The theory of governing by network is a way to address the challenges, and reap the benefits, of social networking.

Examining Trust

As we examine networks, trust theory is important because it has a relationship to dependence, satisfaction and commitment, and it can help with the kind of barriers mentioned above. Trusting relationships involve an ongoing decision to give most people the benefit of the doubt, and trust can be extended even to people one does not know from direct experience. McEvily, Perrone and Zaheer, serving as guest editors, answer the question "Why Trust?" in a special issue on trust in an organizational context (2003). The authors discuss the importance of trust and examine why it is so important "now." They find that a part of the trend is explained by the fact that changes in technology had reconfigured information exchange and the coordination of work across distance and time. Those changes continue today. Focusing on, among other organizational forms, knowledge-intensive organizations, they write:

> "A distinguishing feature of these new organizational forms is that they alter the patterns of interdependencies and the nature and extent of uncertainty. The consequence being that the individuals working in the new organizational forms become more dependent on, and more vulnerable to, the

decisions and actions of others – both preconditions and concomitants of trust (McEvily, Perrone et al. 2003)."

The authors point out that organizational science has made some important advances that promote understanding of the meaning of trust and how it relates to certain factors that characterize organizations. They mention examples of an increasing number of journal articles and special issues (Rousseau, Sitkin et al. 1998, Bachmann, Knights et al. 2001) and books (Gambetta 1988, Kramer 1996, Lane and Bachmann 1998) devoted to the topic of trust in and between organizations. The special issue published seven papers that represent a wide range of methodological approaches, a diverse set of theoretical disciplines, a variety of levels of analysis, and a blend of empirical models (McEvily, Perrone et al. 2003).

Trust is not only important for organizations; it also has individual implications that were mentioned in Chapter 1: dealing with uncertainty and acceptance of vulnerability (Newell and Swan 2000). Luhman (1988) argues that can stimulate engagement activities in spite of uncertainty or risk. Trust is also a multi-dimensional concept where values, attitudes and emotions or moods interact (Newell and Swan 2000). There are three reasons someone may be able to develop trust (Sako 1992):

- Because of a contractual agreement that binds the parties in the relationship;
- Because of a belief in the competencies of those involved; and
- Because of a belief in the goodwill of those involved.

There are other dimensions to consider as well. The research of Dirks and Ferrin has a wide focus and great applicability here, covering trust in organizational settings (2001), using rewards to increase and decrease trust (2003), and examining the effects of third-party relationships on interpersonal trust (2006). A typology distinguishing between deterrence-based trust, knowledge-based trust and identification-based trust was developed in 1992 (Shapiro, Sheppard et al.).

Zucker (1986) argues for a developmental focus, establishing three central mechanisms of trust production: process-based, characteristic-based and institutional-based. Process-based trust focuses on reciprocal, recurring exchanges. Characteristic-based trust is defined by social similarity. Institutional-based trust is determined by expectations embedded in societal norms and structures.

Develop Social Capital

No evaluation of social networking and individual perceptions of performance would be complete without examining social capital theory (Putnam 1993). Social capital theory is a prominent consideration in all social media applications, and is important to any view of performance or behaviors that drive it. The theory's central ideas are that relationships matter and that social networks are a valuable asset (Field 2003). People derive benefits from interaction that builds communities and from commitment that creates ties. This is how we knit a kind of "social fabric." Social capital theory suggests that trust relationships are essential for social networking experiences, building strong ties and a sense of belonging.

Social capital is built between individuals and between organizations. It is all about establishing relationships purposefully and employing them to generate intangible and tangible social, psychological, emotional and economic benefits in short or long terms. Social capital can be examined in terms of five dimensions:

- Networks or lateral associations between individuals and/or groups;
- Reciprocity and expectation;
- Trust and risk based on assumptions;
- Social norms; and
- Personal and collective efficacy.

Social capital and organizational learning have been studied to examine knowledge transfer and perceived organizational performance. Rhodes et al (2008) examined these relationships, integrating organizational learning capability with social capital to shape a holistic knowledge sharing and management enterprise framework. The researchers argued that an integrative model can produce a significant strategy to achieve organizational success. Their results indicate that these dimensions are distinct and have different effects on knowledge transfer.

Examining social capital in the online era requires different sets of scales than have been historically used for these purposes. Researchers argue that existing approaches to studying social capital online have been stymied by importing measurements from older, functionally different media (Williams 2006). Williams (2006) attempts to theorize, create, and validate a series of scales to measure social capital in online and offline contexts, finding 10-item scales that are valid and reliable. The confirmatory factor analysis in that research was primarily concerned with bridging and bonding as two distinct but related dimensions of social capital.

© Can Stock Photo Inc./michaeldb

Bridging and bonding are important dimensions for use in social networking. Robert D. Putnam (1993) defines these kinds of social capital, saying that bonding occurs when people socialize with others who are like them – same age, same race, same religion, and so on. However, Putnam contends, in order to create peaceful societies in a diverse multi-ethnic country, one needs bridging. Bridging is what you do when you make friends with people who may not be like you, like those who don't root for your favorite team, who don't go to your favorite restaurant, or who don't drive your favorite car. Bonding and bridging strengthen each other, which can be seen in social networking. Both types are continuously at play.

Social networking is about accepting the challenge of getting people to believe that online interactions will lead to improvement of their performance, or that they can enhance their life or work in some way. Convincing people that a change may result in some level of performance improvement is no easy task. For instance, a study conducted among 100 international senior executives involved in technological innovation within their firms examined barriers to in-house diffusion of new ideas (Vandermerwe 1987). First among the barriers listed was the difficulty of making observable benefits clear to others. Other barriers mentioned by survey respondents included risks that were perceived as too high, interdepartmental resistance, lack of consensus on benefits, and political and psychological concerns.

================================ ∞ ================================

Food For Thought: Emotional Intelligence

Emotional intelligence (EI) (Cooper 1997) is a theory that organizations can use to determine the desired behaviors for success. EI provides a basis to understand employees, because it is the ability to sense, understand and effectively apply the power and acumen of emotions as a source of human energy, information, trust, creativity and influence. Those who possess emotional intelligence can effectively acknowledge and value feelings in themselves and in others, and can respond to those feelings in an effective way. Paying attention to emotions can save the leader time by directing energies more effectively, and expanding opportunities. Emotional Intelligence has three driving forces: build trusting relationships, increase energy and effectiveness, and create the future. Research shows that emotional intelligence far outweighs IQ and raw brain power as the primary success factor in decision making, creating dynamic organizations, and achieving lifestyle satisfaction and success (Cooper 1997).

================================ ∞ ================================

Whether social capital is achieved through bonding or bridging or some other dimension, it goes hand in hand with trust. It also has relevance to the other theories mentioned earlier: social learning theory, social network analysis, and the Hawthorne effect.

Social Learning

Social learning theory suggests that increased participation and increased modeling may have positive effects on social networking. That means that values are important in making social media participation decisions, and that participation – whether organizational or individual – should be viewed as being capable of satisfying needs in terms of mission accomplishment and productivity.

Social learning theory explains human behavior in terms of four component processes under the umbrella of observational learning, stressing continuous reciprocal interaction between cognitive, behavioral and environmental influences (Bandura 1977):

- Attention, using modeled events and observer characteristics;
- Retention, including symbolic coding, cognitive organization, symbolic rehearsal and motor rehearsal;
- Motor reproduction, including physical capabilities, self-observation of reproduction and accuracy of feedback; and
- Motivation, including external, vicarious and self-reinforcement.

Bandura's guided mastery modeling is beneficial in addressing task breakdowns and structured reinforcement that coincides with social networking interactions. Mastery modeling is used widely to develop intellectual, social, and behavioral competencies, with the best results coming from the use of three elements: skill modeling, guided skill mastery and a transfer program (Bandura 1986). The process begins with modeling of the appropriate skills to convey the basic competencies. General rules and strategies for dealing with different situations are necessary, so people can apply the general rules to specific situations.

Individuals are now equipped with an understanding of the rules, so the next step is to give them guidance and opportunities to perfect their skills. This is done with simulated situations in which they don't have to fear the possibility that they might be inadequately skilled or that they will make mistakes. This modeling and guided performance under simulated conditions has been shown to be an excellent way to create competencies (Wood and Bandura 1989). The skills probably won't be used for a prolonged period unless individuals have a sense that they will be useful skills when put into practice in work situations. Organizations can take these actions in training, but individuals can acquire the skills either through their online interactions or from trial and error in finding what works best.

Therefore, the third requirement for effective mastery modeling is a transfer program aimed at providing self-directed success. People need the experience of enough success with their new set of skills so that they believe equally in themselves and in the value of the new ways of interacting online. At work, an effective transfer program achieves this by allowing the new skills to be employed on the job in situations that are likely to produce good results. At home, people can evaluate their new skills based on increased interactive activity, more likes on Facebook, more likes or profile views on LinkedIn, or more followers on Twitter, for instance.

Porras (1982) suggested that a mastery modeling program can improve not only employee performance and affect morale and productivity in organizations, but it can affect supervisors' skills in a positive way. These improvements can carry over into personal social media activities.

The Porras study showed that supervisors who had the benefit of the modeling program maintained and even improved their supervisory problem-solving skills in ratings provided by their employees. The plant in which the modeling program was applied had a lower absentee rate, lower turnover of employees, and a higher level of productivity in follow-up assessments.

Social learning theory also suggests the use of behavior self-management to affect performance (Davis and Luthans 1980). This approach requires awareness of the contingencies regulating behavior, which is acquired mainly through self-observation and self-monitoring. "Self-monitoring provides the information on the frequency of the behavior and helps define the contingencies [antecedent cues (A), cognitions (O), response-consequences (C)] when they take place (Davis and Luthans 1980)."

Self-monitoring also offers the benefits of objectivity in evaluating behavior and designing an intervention strategy. The goal of the effort is usually to establish a new behavior, increase or maintain an existing behavior, or reduce or eliminate a behavior (Mahoney and Thoresen 1974, Watson and Tharp 1977).

While social learning theory is about modeling, social network analysis is about understanding the dynamics of interaction and making them work in one's favor. It focuses on the primary activities of bonding, bridging and linking among participants to enhance individual performance and promote success of social media activities. Whether the focus is on individuals or organizations, it is important to create a mutual effort of bonding, bridging and linking to ensure that standards, or rules of engagement, are identified, operationalized, and achieved.

Social Network Analysis

Social network analysis is different from social learning theory in that it analyzes shared relationships to drive benefits in a positive direction, instead of creating new skills to improve interaction.

Analysis allows participants to maximize the exchange process, which is intended to maximize benefits and minimize costs, requiring people to weigh the potential benefits and risks of social relationships. When the risks outweigh the rewards, people will terminate or abandon that relationship. Analysis also helps individuals and organizations make the most of communities of interest.

Millen and Fontaine (2003) noted that most people in one study agreed that community activities influence various personal benefits, specifically productivity. That kind of finding could be further development of the work of Dennis and Valacich (1994), part of which addressed synergy. Synergy develops when a participant builds on information provided by another participant to create new ideas, typically because that participant has additional information, different skills, or a different view of the problem. Social media offers individuals and organizations ways to archive shared experiences and then give community members opportunities to recreate that success or to apply the same experience to a new effort.

The Hawthorne Effect

After social network analysis, we turn to the Hawthorne effect, which points out the importance of understanding the focus of social networking activities from "who" is interacting and "what" is the interaction about, and adjusting that focus to "who" is interacting and "what" are the tasks required for success. In other words, successful social media interaction demands that we focus not on what is being said, but on how we can make sure that what we are saying is heard.

Mayo's work with the Hawthorne studies (1949) is helpful in illustrating the need for an understanding of the task at hand and for reinforcement of communication activities. The Hawthorne effect suggests that providing complimentary structure to the networking environment could deliver positive results. Organizations should understand that major findings from Elton Mayo's Hawthorne studies from 1924 to 1932 addressed aligning human resources with organizational factors. Mayo's studies showed that workers respond to group norms, social pressures, and observation (Ivancevich 2008). A group norm is a major factor that the studies have in common with social networking. The way to take advantage of group norms and other similarities is through effective task analyzability practices and structured reinforcement; however, we must first look at radical change.

Withey et al (1983) discussed virtually embedded ties that require tasks that can be easily analyzed in terms of the type of work required, the amount of knowledge matter that is available, a clear progression of how the work should be done, and easy access to information on relevant procedures and practices.

Social networking represents radical change, so it is important to examine the change process as separate components. There are three critical steps required to manage radical change: receptivity, mobilization, and learning (Huy 1999). Receptivity is a person's willingness to consider change and it is characterized as both a state and a process. At any fixed point in time, a person can accept the need for the proposed change if there is an interpretive, attitudinal state on the cognitive and emotional level.

Mobilization is about people taking concrete action in the direction of an intended change. Attitudes can vary from resigned to passive acceptance to enthusiastic endorsement.

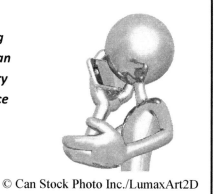

© Can Stock Photo Inc./LumaxArt2D

The concrete action a person takes in the direction of change is mobilization. This is the process of rallying and propelling different segments of the organization to undertake joint action and to realize common change goals (Huy 1999).

Receptivity and mobilization are linked to, or lead to, learning. Individuals learn by thinking and then acting, using the outcome of action to revise his or her belief system (Kim 1993). Receptivity is an observed change, where individuals exhibit various stages of willingness to accept the proposed change. Change attitudes can vary from resigned, passive acceptance to enthusiastic endorsement.

Huy's (1999) characterization of the radical change process maintains that when receptivity leads to motivation, individuals and organizations also can learn from the outcomes of the changes they enact. Learning provides a feedback loop from the outcomes of behavioral change back to receptivity. In other words, the learning process is a beginning, but that beginning leads back to using that process to sustain receptivity at the desired level. In turn, sustained receptivity at the correct level leads to continued mobilization and so forth. All of the characteristics of radical change are important as one evaluates how to enhance the social networking experience.

This theoretical examination is by no means exhaustive. The growing volumes of information include more on social networking (Cerulo 1990, Zack and McKenney 1995, Fowler, Lawrence et al. 2004, Chung, Hossain et al. 2007), trust (Newell and Swan 2000, Nyhan 2000), measuring performance or productivity (Davis and Luthans 1980, Bearman, Guynup et al. 1985, Otis 2007, Akdere and Roberts 2008), and capacity or skill building (Shetzer 1993, Segrest, Domke-Damonte et al. 1998, Eastin and LaRose 2000, Erickson and Jacoby 2003) for instance. However, the social networking literature is primarily descriptive and categorizing without providing value-creation and value-capturing strategies.

Individuals and organizations can use the social media theories outlined above to achieve the best, most successful social media experience.

Chapter 3: Social Media Engagement

∞

Engagement

This chapter is about engagement. The task is to make sense of the way people connect, and then find ways to help them discover like-minded individuals and share valuable connections using the social media platform of choice. We are in search of truly unfettered trust, and that search requires that we find trust in those we might not trust otherwise. It also requires that we create social capital to exchange valuable content in any number of exciting interactions. Social Media 4EVR is about determining where you want to go with your social networking participation and then leveraging a plan that will get you there. No one wants to post something on social media that no one pays attention to. So our engagement strategy is to look at our community, listen to what they're saying, understand what they need, and then exchange valuable content with them. Not an easy task, but well worth the time and effort to create a place for yourself in your community of interest. Success, then, requires that we identify the "why" of social networking participation while focusing on creating social capital. Next, we must evaluate and/or revise our online presence to be as effective, and visible, as we feel comfortable with. We must communicate on one or more social media platforms, because all of our target audience won't "reside" in the same place. These actions lead to development of an effective engagement strategy.

∞

Now that you have some history and a basis of social media theory, we need to lay out our road map for social networking success. Successful engagements are important, and they must be based on effective use of the pillars of social media to deliver and receive valuable expectations, values and returns within our communities of interest. The four pillars of social media that we will discuss in the next chapter establish tools we use to interact in the digital conversation, allowing us to focus on the benefits people get from engaging with each other.

Engagement is about enhancing performance by mastering the challenges we face every day in life and online. There are many challenges, starting with seeking alignment of your goal with your intended audience or community. Engagement requires attempting to coordinate all of your social media activity so your digital "self" looks the same across platforms. Successful interaction requires avoiding communication meltdown where you are overwhelmed by your activity. It's important to manage the tension that can come with collaboration that doesn't make sense or gets you in trouble. Finally, overcoming limitations of your social networking abilities and knowledge are vital to successful engagements.

© Can Stock Photo Inc./niloo

An end state can help create a road map for participation.

Of course, having clear goals and objectives for social networking and using some type of plan to guide your efforts is always recommended, but there's more to this social networking game. The best start is to determine your end state and make sure you can get there. If you've already started, then analyze your end state and determine if you're headed there. Or, if you've already started and can't determine your end state, it's time to take a break and set one. The end state allows you to devise a road map to guide your efforts.

That roadmap allows you to use the end state or mission to determine the process you follow, allowing the necessary change from the tradition of deciding on a process and then trying to fit it to a mission or end state. Keep in mind that if you're working social media for your organization, this end state idea is about asking the right questions about the outcome-based value proposition, or public value, that the organization seeks. The personal and/or organizational approach suggested allows the destination, not the path, to be the focus around which the components and interactions of the network are built (Goldsmith and Eggers 2004).

Select your network partners wisely to ensure you can build long-standing, mutually beneficial relationships. The focus of these interactions is shared value that creates ties that endure because of dependable communication channels, coordinated activities between network participants, and the establishment of trusting relationships. Beyond just the technology, social networking success also requires vigilance in addressing interactivity with the people you value, examining and improving your processes constantly, and aligning values and trust to complement each other.

Finding Value

These concerns and responsibilities, when managed effectively, can open the door to the enormous value available to participants. The value is available because of the varied and unlimited points of personal and professional contact that can be translated into useful responses by everyone involved in the network, allowing each participant to adjust their responses appropriately. Social media activities are helped by creating linkages between social networking and performance to achieve the greatest interaction possible. This is the way to create collaboration and/or interaction.

For example, a 2005 dissertation (Golbeck) employed two applications to rate levels of trust and use trust-based ratings as collaborative filtering techniques. "Trust was defined as follows: Alice trusts Bob if she commits to an action based on a belief that Bob's future actions will lead to a good outcome (Golbeck 2005)." This work was directed specifically at trust in web-based social networks, how it can be computed, and how it can be used in creating applications. The research involved a survey of web-based social networks to understand their scope, the types of relationship information available, and the current state of trust. This example illustrates how powerful trust can be in getting users to participate in social networking, and in showing them how they might benefit personally and professionally from the activity.

The context of those digital engagements relies on an understanding of social capital; that's really what we're building. Building social capital is one way to address collective problems quickly and solve them easily. Those who build trust and social capital tend to be the catalysts for ensuring communities advance in pursuit of their stated goals. Social capital can also illustrate how active and trusting connections with others widen our awareness and reveal commonalities in society that often prove beneficial. Social media tools are the fastest way to arrive at these outcomes.

The networked approach to social engagement outlined to this point seeks a focus on active involvement that develops real relationships with the public or a community of interest. Engagement requires becoming more involved in your current community of interest, getting involved in existing communities, and fostering collaborative interactions.

When you engage, you want to deliver great content that advances your networking initiatives. You want to generate interest that leads to ongoing communications. Engagement should also deliver social capital to your intended audience, and return social capital to you via the ensuing collaborations and conversations.

As you evaluate or measure your engagement, don't focus on numbers alone, ask yourself some very pointed questions. What is the relationship of your outcomes to your objectives? Are there any events created as a result of your engagement activities? Do inquiries from your intended audience request substantive information or services from you? Go beyond the numbers and you should see value and social capital. If you don't find value and social capital, refocus your engagements or change your objectives to get meaningful outcomes.

Build More Capital

Now that we've defined engagement, let's talk about social capital. Social capital exists between people and organizations and is all about establishing relationships purposefully and employing them to generate intangible and tangible social, psychological, emotional and economic benefits in short or long terms.

Companies are interested in social networking because of its potential to deliver measurable benefits like innovation, effective marketing, rapid access to information, lower costs and higher revenues.

In its Fall 2009 application and usage report, Palo Alto Networks (2009) reported that an Enterprise 2.0 survey showed that the top three business benefits identified were knowledge sharing (60%), reduced effort in information gathering (50%), and improved efficiency/speed of delivery (35%). Companies can address their communication, information, entertainment or transaction purposes through integrating social media platforms across the business enterprise. Those corporations may find compelling benefits through the creation and implementation of a social media plan, which leads us to engagement.

Engagement is the conscious attempt to gain attention and reputation. The process begins with an understanding of what you have to offer or, put another way, with the knowledge about what can be shared that is worthy of giving and receiving input. The social networking process has some distinct steps you'll want to follow. They are creating compelling content, fostering adoption or participation, filtering incoming and outgoing information, and maintaining levels of activity. Along the way, you'll need to determine appropriate online spaces and channels, evaluating each social media space. When evaluating a social media space, you want to understand the audience you are engaging. Finally, set some goals and milestones to develop participation opportunities that will last.

Improving Participation

There is another way to look at participation. Three things can influence successful social networking:

- Concrete incentives to participate in the kind of social media one values;

- Improved definition of the activities required through task analyzability; and

- Continuous feedback through structured reinforcement.

Success is based on normative practices as well as relationships that build trust, foster interaction, and address participant needs. There are other commonalities, such as how social networking stresses focused interaction between individuals (Sabatini 2009) and how individual performance concerns task-specific interaction (Ivancevich 2008). Further, in an organizational sense, Hatala and Fleming (2007) argue for a social network perspective that is characterized by "centrality (betweenness, closeness, degree), position (structural), strength of ties (strong/weak, weighted/discrete), cohesion (groups, cliques) and division (structural holes, partition)."

Individual performance is based on somewhat related constructs, such as social interaction for centrality (Ivancevich 2008), involvement and need fulfillment for position (Mayo 1949), formal and informal ties for strength of ties (Ivancevich 2008), two-way personal selection for cohesion (Mayo 1949), and self-importance for division (Mayo 1949). Self-importance may create instances where the individual's inward focus contributes to disconnected activities in terms of the organization and its mission.

Task analyzability, as defined by Perrow (1967), refers to the way that individuals are able to respond to problems encountered in the process of task completion. Analyzable tasks are useful because they have predetermined responses to potential problems or well-known procedures, allowing outcomes that can be easily understood. Task analyzability seeks information in four areas (Withey, Daft et al. 1983):

- Clear definitions for accomplishing the major types of work;
- Clearly defined and available body of knowledge;
- Clear sequence of steps for tasks; and
- Reliance on policy and procedures.

There are also relevant questions to be asked in the interest of task analyzability:

- Is there a clear way to do the major types of work (conduct activities)?
- Is there a clearly defined body of knowledge matter available?
- Is there an understandable sequence of steps to follow?
- Is there actual reliance on established procedures and practices?

If there is good task analyzability, the next consideration for improving performance is structured reinforcement. Continuous reinforcement is important because learning experts believe that it is the most important principle of learning (Ivancevich 2008). A structured reinforcement plan that provides feedback during critical performance times allows real-time information concerning whether the relevant actions are correct or incorrect.

© Can Stock Photo Inc./nmarques74

Structured reinforcement is characterized by on-demand training, real-time results, ongoing recognition and reinforcement tied to specific actions. It also includes assistance to continue value-plus actions or eliminate value-minus actions.

Structured reinforcement can be accomplished through the use of performance support tools (PSTs), which provide workers with on-the-job help, advice, information, examples or assurance. These can be job aids that remind us of things we have to do, recipes or assembly instructions, or even online resources to help us get information or solve problems.

Like electronic performance support systems (EPSSs), PSTs describe the technological tools that help people make decisions, plan for activities, and perform tasks (Paino and Rossett 2008). This would require identifying the relevant PSTs for assisting employees with their most critical tasks. The idea is to go beyond simply identifying others who are engaged in the same specialty area and who are taking on the same tasks. The goal is to identify the necessary steps to be taken and determine whether the employee's "right-now actions" are, as stated above, value-plus or value-minus.

If one wants a true test of how the social networking effort is progressing, virtually embedded ties can be used to track and measure workflow and interactions. Fowler, Lawrence and Morse (2004) define virtually embedded ties as linkages that are initiated and maintained through electronic technologies and that provide distinctive solutions to the same problems with exchange relationships that are addressed by socially embedded ties. The authors suggest that this approach allows managers to draw on linkages that have distinctive characteristics that draw on the speed, efficiency, and global reach of contemporary technologies to mitigate the factors that can make arm's-length ties problematic.

Virtually embedded ties have three principal components: trust, fine-grained information transfer, and joint problem-solving arrangements. These ties have the ability to regulate expectations and behaviors of exchange partners. They enable embedded ties to overcome critical exchange-related problems that arm's-length ties cannot address effectively – opportunism, uncertainty and complexity (Williamson 1975, Williamson 1985).

Of course, formal incentives, task analyzability activities, structured reinforcement concerns, and virtually embedded ties are primarily organizational-level tools and techniques. However, individuals may use these constructs to their benefit. All that's required is to understand the basis for these considerations. For the individual, formal incentives are ways to self-motivate and motivate others to the communication activity. Task analyzability is about making a critical analysis of activities to determine the benefits they may deliver. Structured reinforcement is about getting help and/or feedback concerning the activity while it is in progress. Individuals already benefit from virtually embedded ties; these are the linkages that are created and maintained based on one's social network connections and online activities.

That's what engagement is about – finding value, building capital and improving participation. Done well, you'll reap plenty of benefits in your social networking activities driven by staying focused on the context of applying social media pillars and by engaging appropriately to gain adoption and trust within your community of interest. Adoption should be a by-product of good bookmarking and tagging practices, and of adding people to your social media groups. Attention and reputation should reasonably offer continuing collaboration activities.

Introduction to Social Media and Social Networking

Dr. Michael A. Brown Sr. with Tracy Schario, APR

If regular media is a one-way street, then social media is a two-way street that delivers unlimited ability to comment and discuss and offers a fast way to read the newspaper or digest a TV report.

So, we must draw a correlation between social media and social networking. According to Matt Goddard, chief executive officer, R2i.ntegrated, social media is about using different tools, or platforms, to communicate socially. The tools allow us to communicate and store information without limitations of location or time. Anyone can connect with anyone anywhere if both parties are participating in social media.

Social networking is people getting together to share experiences and get advice to help them make better decisions. Also, we reach out to people so that we can reduce risk in personal and/or business decisions by taking advantage of their expertise.

Corporate social media focus
- Control and expand your brand;
- Relay messages quickly;
- Generate conversation and gather feedback;
- Build relationships;
- Foster information sharing among employees; and
- Affect employee communication, retention and morale.

Available benefits
- Increase traffic and interaction on your site;
- Use interaction to ensure you understand your audience;
- Find new ways to collect and share information;
- Reach people who are unavailable by other means;
- Create buy-in for a brand or product; and
- Develop transparency with important internal and external publics.

Short list of social media platforms
- Facebook: A website where you communicate with friends and family, share photos or links, play social games, search and chat interactively with your friends/co-workers/acquaintances.
- Twitter: An online social networking and micro-blogging service that enables its users to send tweets, which are like status updates or

links on Facebook; they're just limited to 140 characters. You can follow anyone and anyone can follow you, and you don't have to do anything to make this happen.

- LinkedIn: A social networking website which focuses on the kind of networking that helps people get jobs. Your profile on LinkedIn is actually your résumé. People refer to this site as the business version of Facebook.
- Flickr: Host images and video with an online community. Users share and embed personal photographs. This is widely used by bloggers to host images embedded in blogs and social media.
- YouTube: A video-sharing website where users can upload, view and share videos. The site displays a wide variety of user-generated video content, including movie clips, TV clips, and music videos, as well as amateur content such as video blogging, short original videos, and educational videos.
- Google+: A website very similar to Facebook where you can post your status and share photos, videos and links. The main difference is that you can create "circles" of people (i.e. family, friends, co-workers) which will determine who can see the items that you post.
- Pinterest: A pin board-style photo sharing website that allows users to create and manage theme-based image collections such as events, interests, hobbies, and more. Users can browse other pin boards for inspiration, "re-pin" images to their own pin boards, or "like" photos.
- Instagram: The website describes it this way. "Instagram is a fast, beautiful and fun way to share your life with friends and family. Take a picture or video, choose a filter to transform its look and feel, then post to Instagram — it's that easy. You can share to Facebook, Twitter, Tumblr and more. It's a new way to see the world."
- Blogs: A blog (web log) is a discussion or informational site published on the Internet consisting of discrete entries, or posts, typically displayed in reverse chronological order (the most recent post appears first).

The full list of social media platforms continues to grow at a rapid pace.

∞

Chapter 4: Four Pillars of Social Media

Apply Social Media Strategy

This chapter is about communication, collaboration, education and entertainment – the four pillars of social media strategy. We discuss the four pillars as a framework to achieve EVR, or expectation, value and return on investment of time and attention. Intended expectations include two-way unfettered communication, education of someone or some community of interest, and improving someone's day – or making it less bad. It all requires the quality content that can be offered through social networking. The value to which we refer is need satisfaction: receiving information, collaborating, collecting information that is more difficult or time-consuming to get elsewhere, and easing someone's mind through a valuable exchange or interaction. The return we seek can be creating an "open door" for information and collaboration, leveraging different learning styles and venues, or creating ways for me to entertain you and for you to entertain me back. Successfully defining and using the four pillars of social media is very important to quality participation.

∞

Developing an understanding of the four pillars – communication, collaboration, education and entertainment – is the perfect way to set yourself up for social media success. The pillars can be helpful regardless of your desired end state, whether you're building a trusted environment, connecting with a new person or group for short- or long-term purposes, or working to become a thought leader in your industry or community. One or all of the pillars can be in play at any time, but it's important to pick one to lead your effort and be consistent with it.

The best use of the four pillars, however, comes with an understanding of the interactive dialogue atmosphere that is social networking. For instance, Kwon & Wen (2010) employed a technology acceptance model (TAM) based instrument to measure perceived usefulness, perceived ease of use, and perceived encouragement, all useful considerations in social media activities and applications. Perceived usefulness refers to the degree to which the user believes that using the technology will improve his or her work performance. This focuses on the motivational and value-added aspects of social media. Perceived usefulness refers to capabilities that reinforce good performance in various ways within an organizational context; these capabilities can be used advantageously. A system high in perceived usefulness reinforces the user's belief in the existence of a positive use-performance relationship.

Perceived ease of use refers to a person's perception of how little (or how much) effort is required to use the technology. In this way, the "work" involved derives value from the individual's assessment of the process of using the system and from the commitment required to participate. Commitment is viewed in terms of time, attention and the individual or company's ultimate assessment of the participation outcome.

Perceived encouragement can be an individual consideration, but most experts consider this to be the way that organizational encouragement to participate affects human performance. That refers to the behavior exhibited in participation, how individuals make the decision on whether or not to participate, and how much value can be found in outcomes of that participation. Perceived encouragement is about expression, literally and verbally, of support for the social media enterprise (Kwon and Wen 2010), and that support is a critical consideration in the quest for successful digital interactions. Kwon and Wen (2010) argued that encouragement is a sort of intangible social support that provides a specific individual with psychological wellness. People can avoid negative stimuli or recover from undesired states based on perceived encouragement. The researchers focused on literal encouragement through a blogging concept, examining how people perceive others' encouraging expression and analyzing whether that distinction was more critical than how the person expressed his or her willingness to encourage a different person.

Understanding perceived usefulness, perceived ease of use, and perceived encouragement provides a foundation for use of the social media pillars mentioned earlier. This foundation facilitates and invigorates communication. Communication is about informing the public and it must be a two-way process where you learn and understand what others are saying about you, making sure people are sharing the messages you intended, and ensuring you are having valuable interactions. Of course, a solid personal or professional brand and message are vital to the communication effort. This brand addresses who you are, what you believe in and what you have to offer in communicating these things to other people. Communication is interactive listening.

What does interactive listening mean? One view is eloquently explained in "Listen Closely: How Social Businesses Succeed" in Public Relations Society of America (PRSA) *Public Relations Strategist*, excellently penned by Phyllis Fair and Tyler Durham (2013). They make great points about the importance of listening in social media activities.

The authors discussed the results of a Ketchum and FedEx Social Business Study, listing several takeaways:

- Look beyond connecting with people and focus on building meaningful relationships with key stakeholders;
- Develop a strong capability to listen to and understand all audiences;
- Trust and empower employees and strive for increased transparency in activities;
- Coordinate the organization's messages and goals into a unified voice across all channels; and
- Be flexible to adapt to and respond to stakeholders in real time.

This reference reinforces the need to take advantage of unfettered, two-way communication with the audiences that are important to you. The beauty of social networking lies not only in its immediacy but in its ability to get and give feedback in real time.

This participation vision is based on real findings from social media experts in the field. The social media revolution is upon us, and it's not slowing down. Organizations, whether they want to or not, are going social on the inside, so it's important to listen to the digital conversation at every opportunity. Finally, strategic listening allows people and organizations to engage stakeholders and friends using the channels they prefer.

There are great tools at your disposal to unleash communication and improve your listening ability. Will you accept the challenge?

Collaboration

Collaboration is all about effective interaction with people and organizations that matter in terms of your desired end state. How do you engage them and, when you do, what sort of participation do you want from them? To figure it out, you need a plan, and you need to be able to deliver the WIIFM – What's In It For Me (Them) – at the outset. You will also need to decide what avenues or tools are most appropriate for the engagement with your target audience. Wikis and online forums are just two examples of ways for you to get started. Collaboration is about forming the connection.

The connection can be personal or professional, and it is based on trust. For instance, given the current social networking environment, organizations increasingly provide "social media time" as part of processes to create new business, enhance innovation, and improve the work and personal lives of employees. Those processes require that organizations seek interactions that are administratively effective and professionally accountable. Therefore, social networking is a two-step, voluntary process where people accept or reject participation, and then determine levels of activity that suit their needs and/or lifestyles. Collaboration requires that you make the decisions necessary to facilitate your participation based on your personal social media plan or desires.

For more on collaboration, see Pat Weber's article at the end of this chapter.

Education

Now let's look at education. What about education as the guiding force for social networking? This can be tough, because you need to have expertise in the area you're discussing, your audience needs to know about and/or acknowledge that expertise, and you need a call to action that moves them to some activity. Sharing information is important, as is the WIIFM. One motivational approach would be to offer some kind of incentive to early responders – gift certificate, free whitepaper on a valued topic, etc. You can also educate your audience through blogs, which are considered the most influential social media tool in existence today. Education, then, is about information exchange.

================ ∞ ================

4 Pillars:

Communication, Collaboration, Education, Entertainment

Keys to Effective Use

Enabling conditions

Communication champions

Information appropriateness

Access to information

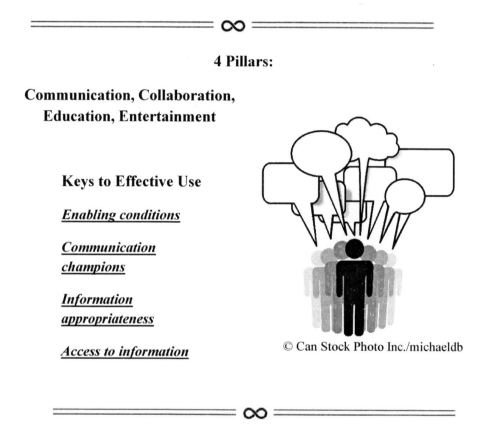

© Can Stock Photo Inc./michaeldb

================ ∞ ================

The key to information exchange is your educational intent. Trying to conduct free and open communication is very different in approach and information sharing than trying to find or impress potential employers. Your success in sharing educational content lies in being clear on your approach and in offering value for both sender and receiver. That's the challenge.

Entertainment is the fourth pillar available for you to leverage. Most savvy social media gurus would make YouTube one of the first things mentioned here, because people want to hear and watch good stories, they want to laugh, they want to be inspired to dance, and they want to see something amazing. That's why videos are so valuable; they entertain easily and become part of the conversation quickly. They are memorable ways to communicate your message on a regular basis. This can be a valuable tool in your social media kit, so getting familiar with processes to produce video content is a very good idea. But entertainment is about so much more.

Real entertainment value lies in providing something that might be considered a train wreck. You know the story. There's a blog or a tweet or a video that I don't know why I'm watching, but I can't turn away. I don't really know its value, but *I MUST WATCH IT, I MUST READ IT!* If you can conquer that outside-the-box dilemma, you'll be an entertainment guru in no time.

Regardless of which pillar you use, it will be important to create enabling conditions that allow success. There are four keys that can facilitate those conditions. The first key is facilitating dialogue with an organized and capable community. The community of interest must be engaged in ongoing digital conversations that create shared value and build social capital. The second key, communication champions, is vital to keeping conversations alive. Communication champions are not only engaged in the conversation, they energize it and even take it to other communities to inject other points of view.

The third key, information appropriateness, both contextual and cultural, focuses on ensuring conversations are relevant and appropriate for the community of interest. Relevance and appropriateness are based on demographic values of the community, as well as cultural considerations. In other words, the group should act and communicate in ethical and transparent ways. The fourth key is access to information, which is crucial for the other keys to work. If your community doesn't know why, when, where or how you're posting information, communication will suffer. Also, if you use, for instance, an RSS feed that doesn't work, no value can be exchanged.

Use these keys, enabling conditions, communication champions, information appropriateness, and access to information, to energize your strategy. They are also relevant regardless of which of the four pillars, or which combination of them, you employ.

Communication, collaboration, education or entertainment: which is right for you? You will see in later chapters that your intent, your personal profile, and your expectation of participation in terms of value received and return on investment are the keys to which pillar will be the foundation for your efforts.

∞

Collaboration and Social Media

By Patricia Weber

Collaborating isn't a new business phenomenon. Consider this almost every day scenario in almost any town:

You check in for your appointment with the friendly receptionist at your hair salon. Then on turning around from the conversation to take a seat you notice a flyer on their counter that catches your attention.

But it isn't anything about the salon services at all. It's a full color glossy brochure with all the details about a local community theatre upcoming play.

Because you are a long term and loyal customer to the salon, you pick it up to take it with you while you wait. You read it and even consider going to one of the showings of the play. Or you know a friend who could be interested so you fold the flyer up to take with you when you leave.

You've experienced collaboration by design: a couple of local businesses work together to mutual benefit. There's no doubt someone approached the hair salon owner to help spread the word they needed to get out in this influential manner.

It happens frequently with social media. You discover someone online or a business who you respect and who can influence you, who is pointing you in the direction of someone else's product or online an upcoming event or recent blogging post. That's more collaboration by design.

The most valuable part of collaborating with online social media tools is as long as you have a presence online, and others are finding you, you can either facilitate or be invited to participate to reach a global community.

Why collaborate using social media? Because the world needs savvy people to reach out, spread good news, create ideas, make good offers, share valuable products and more. Purposeful collaboration is one of the fundamental pillars of using online social media to mutual advantage.

It can be a large company working with a smaller one to who some part of a project is outsourced. Then the smaller company may boost the amount of or quality of work. Size of organizations is usually irrelevant because collaborating brings distinct benefits to all parties.

How do you collaborate successfully? Networking is at the heart of collaborating online, and it requires useful tools much like standard office workers use when at different locations. Before you consider collaboration, consider including these typical ideas.

Networking. Collaborating starts with effective networking. Integral to effective networking is being adept in moving the conversation along. Today the options available to do this means you can start with email then move the conversation to Skype or Google+ Hangouts. Being able to meet in-person virtually with tools like this is a helpful substitute for meeting in person.

Agreement. Every day, people online are collaborating to exchange blog posts, participate in a study and create new products. Depending on the depth of collaborating, some kind of term of agreement may be wise. Being a guest blogger for someone is rather limited in scope but participating with someone on an expert panel means more considerations.

Be human. Being online means there are both individual and more cultural differences to consider. Whether it's business or a social cause, collaborating means working together toward common goals. The benefit of innovation in what comes out of collaborating hinges on the trust, understanding and cooperation in personal interactions.

Collaboration is as old and new as science. Social media ends up debunking some scientific beliefs, starting with Charles Darwin's theory of survival of the fittest. Gregg Braden, American author known for bridging science to the new world, states there are more than 400 other scientific studies to support the human predisposition toward cooperation and mutual aid. Because social media collaboration supports a new world of cooperation, it may be continuous proof that humans are wired to benefit from collaboration.

About the Author:
As an internationally recognized authority for the introvert, Patricia Weber supports and inspires introverts and baby boomers to live life at full throttle. Her services help her clients in learning to speak with more confidence, deliver effective presentations, increase sales and networking results and take on leadership roles more often. Some of her books are on Amazon for Kindle http://amazon.com/author/patriciaweber. She blogs at http://www.patricia-weber.com.

∞

Chapter 5: Building Your Brand

∞

Demonstrate Who You Are

This chapter is about building your brand. Who are you? What is important to you? What do you have to offer others in the way of information sharing? What communities do you seek? These are but a few of the important questions our personal and professional brand should answer for people we encounter. Done well, they will be answered without those we contact having to ask the questions. Our brand is our company billboard or website, and it should be alive across all platforms on which we participate. Others can compare their own likes and dislikes and analyze whether we are the like-minded soul they seek. This is by no means easy, and Social Media 4EVR stresses that brand should be interwoven with end state and with the plan of action. Staying on message and on plan ensures brand durability, visibility, consistency, relevance, and a whole host of other considerations. When we brand, we are using a word or image to identify a person or organization or product – or all three. A brand separates us and helps people remember us. More than that, you want a brand that promises quality and reputation to the public in which you operate. Remember, people are busy and tend to follow what they are familiar with. If they have a good experience, and if that experience is consistently good, they will move from remembering your brand to achieving a sense of belonging with your brand. Social media success in branding comes when we develop effective personal and corporate strategies. Most important, be true to your personal brand at all times.

∞

Branding is important because it can say so much about who you are and reveal your expertise. It's important to understand that there are differences between personal brand and corporate brand, and there are differences in the way to build each one. Personal and corporate branding can complement or conflict with each other, so social media adventurers should pay strict attention to how each is employed.

Let's start with a discussion about community building. This is where you'll introduce, nurture and solidify your brand.

Many corporations encourage and are even enthusiastic about employees who use social networking both at work and at home. Corporations, however, have to be consistently concerned about the risks involved in using social media tools, because there is always great potential for getting signals crossed. The signals are about the characterization of individual participation, ensuring there is clear delineation of comment and identity between what is personal, what is professional, what is public and what is private. In the end, a major consideration is about who has reasonable responsibility to share information.

The Department of Defense (DOD) has many great examples of social media and social networking. The DOD has an online hub at http://www.defense.gov/socialmedia/ that lets one know that social media is an integral part of operations. The Army, for instance, has a social media handbook that you can access and use as a guide to DOD Internet services and Internet-based capabilities.

The Navy's social media handbook has guidelines for Sailors and Navy personnel, professional standards and conduct for command leadership, and guidelines for command social media. Perhaps most valuable is the checklist for establishing a command social media presence. All this information is accessible via the DOD social media hub.

The focus of DOD social media efforts is to make information readily accessible on a global scale so that military members and their families can use social media responsibly and effectively, both in official and unofficial capacities. The hub has education and training, terms of service agreements, site registry, and policies for everyone and anyone to use.

If you're seeking the latest on DOD activities, you can visit "Social Media @ DOD." Here you will find a summary that spans the services for all things social media. There is information about connecting with American Forces Press Service and the Pentagon Channel, for example. This is an effective one-stop shop for social media participants.

DOD is not the only entity doing great things. Another example is Nordstrom's Social Networking Guidelines and you can find the full text of that document at: http://shop.nordstrom.com/c/social-networking-guidelines. The company wants employees to talk to their managers and leaders prior to participating in social media. Nordstrom asks employees to adhere to the following guidelines:

- Use good judgment;
- Be respectful;
- Be responsible and ethical;
- Be humble;
- Be a good listener; and
- Avoid conflicts of interest.

Nordstrom mitigates risk through a common sense approach to information sharing, asking employees not to share confidential information. Employees are also asked not to share private and personal information—"yours, customers' and co-workers'." Further, Nordstrom wants employees to be cautious with respect to images and non-company websites. The Nordstrom policy excels in common sense because it acknowledges that something could go wrong, and discusses mitigation strategies.

For instance, the policy suggests that employees ensure that they correct any mistake they make immediately, and clearly state what was done to fix it. Also, Nordstrom says, "If it's a MAJOR mistake (e.g., exposing private customer or employee information or reporting confidential information), please let your manager know immediately so we can take the proper steps to help minimize the impact it may have."

This is great guidance. The key to success is having employees who protect the corporate brand, use corporate messages, and separate corporate and personal identities in simple, straightforward ways.

When working on personal branding, it is crucial to stay away from even the appearance of representing your job or company in your social networking efforts. During personal branding, your thoughts and actions are your own. That's why it a good idea to have a disclaimer in all of your personal efforts to establish this fact. Something like:

"The opinions expressed are my own."

Corporate branding, on the other hand, energizes the organization's name by marrying it with favorable advertising and customer base-building efforts. It attempts to either spark an immediate recognition when one sees or hears the company name and logo, or it strives to make the company a symbol of success or happiness in the minds of consumers.

Personal Branding

Let's get back to the personal touch. Your personal brand is important, because it embodies the experiences, positions, contributions and friendships you make throughout your personal and professional life. Your personal brand is a statement that tells people who you are and why they should connect with you, or why you want to connect with them. It speaks to similarities as well as differences, so the audience can make judgments about participating with you.

That's why you must capture your personal brand and use it to your best advantage, and social networking is the best way to do that. First, create the profile you intend to create and manage it. If you have several profiles for whatever reason, ensure there's a common thread so you exude consistency and sincerity across social media platforms. You need a strategic online presence that will help you in your social media activities.

In the book *"Putting the Public Back in Public Relations,"* the authors use LinkedIn as an example of the power of social media. The authors say "LinkedIn will serve you well, enabling you to manage a virtual Rolodex, cultivate relationships, find people you need to know, promote your business and area of expertise, ask questions to crowd-source qualified responses, and help valuable contacts find you" (Solis and Breakenridge 2009).

Make your profile effective by demonstrating that you have something to offer. To do this, make sure you know what you're talking about when you post, getting help from other knowledgeable sources along the way. It's also important to know why the information you post matters and to be able to deliver that rationale to your audience.

If you can tell a story that clearly demonstrates who is affected and how the information can help or enrich them, you're starting to win the communication challenge. Once you have the personal brand created, use it to determine your value proposition and humanize and personalize your stories (posts) for your audiences.

Create interaction by identifying who you want to contact and determine how they like to receive information. Read and watch their work so you can keep the two-way exchange alive. Continue to monitor the dialogue and follow some simple rules of engagement: listen, learn, respect, and share.

Know with whom you'll network. There are some key questions you can ask:

- Who will you be?
- What will you contribute?
- Who do you want to follow? Follow back?
- Who do you want to engage?
- Who do you want to influence?
- Who do you want sharing your content?

Build your personal brand with sincerity and consistency. You can decide how open you want to be, but when you venture out to invigorate your brand, be sure to be compelling, honest, open and factual.

For more on building brand and community, see Steve Radick's article at the end of this chapter.

Corporate Branding

If corporate branding is successful, a consumer will hear or see the name of the company and associate it with a unique value and positive experiences. No matter what product or service the corporation offers, the corporate name is always an influence. Coca-Cola, for instance, has a powerful corporate brand that focuses on the strength of the name as much as the features of any Coca-Cola products. The advantages to good corporate branding include easier advertising recognition, positive reactions from consumers, familiarity with products, and an ability to drive cost based on popularity and recognition.

When building and delivering your brand, always remember the importance of trust. Trust is crucial to any social networking activity. For businesses, intra-organizational trust is important. This is the trust people in an organization have in one another that creates and nurtures social bonds and collaboration in social networking activities.

Intra-organizational trust is a vital part of achieving collective receptivity to and exploitation of interactions in social networking. It energizes the cognitive, affective and moral dimensions of digital conversations and describes the perceived intent and behaviors of organizational members.

Individuals should look to trust in general, which is necessary for developing relationship dependence, satisfaction and commitment. Trusting relationships allow individuals to make the ongoing decisions necessary to give most people the benefit of the doubt, and it can be extended even to people one does not know from direct experience. Relevant literature across several disciplines supports the widespread influence of trust.

Talking about trust requires an understanding of two issues central to communication interaction. The first involves trust as a means for dealing with uncertainty. The second focuses on trust and acceptance of vulnerability (Newell and Swan 2000). Luhman (1988) argues that trust occurs in situations of risk and uncertainty: "A system requires trust as an input condition in order to stimulate supportive activities in situations of uncertainty or risk."

Luhmann suggests that trust is an attitudinal mechanism that allows individuals to subjectively assess whether or not to expose themselves to situations where there may not be an acceptable trade-off in terms of possible damage versus received advantage. The attitude develops when individuals have accepted vulnerability to others.

Trust is also a multi-dimensional concept where values, attitudes and emotions or moods interact (Newell and Swan 2000). There are three reasons someone may be able to develop trust (Sako 1992):

- Because of a contractual agreement that binds the parties in the relationship;
- Because of a belief in the competencies of those involved; and
- Because of a belief in the goodwill of those involved.

However they are developed, trusting relationships are vital to collaboration in organizations, or to seeking out people who will enrich one's personal social networking. Developing that trust is central to the overall social media adventure.

∞

Start Community with Role Models, Not Influencers
By Steve Radick

Make friends, not ads. ™

That's the message that greeted me when I first walked into the lobby on my first day at Cramer-Krasselt. It was refreshing to walk into a marketing agency and see them so overtly eschew traditional advertising ("look at me!! Come buy my stuff!! Now! Now! Now!") and traditional PR ("we're the world's leading provider of innovative solutions...") and embrace the increasingly deepening relationships that brands have with their consumers. I now realize that this is much more than a tagline - it's the future of branding.

People aren't stupid. They recognize, ignore, and actively avoid advertising like never before. Brands are learning that the hard sell is actually driving more customers away than it's bringing in. While brands may intuitively realize this, they struggle to actually put this thinking into action. Rather than thinking about the latest marketing fad, viral video, or influencer outreach programs, brands have to take a step back, reevaluate who they are, what they stand for, and what value they offer their customers.

You've heard of Pinterest, right? If you haven't, there's a good chance it inspired that casserole your wife made last night or those shoes she just bought. This massively popular site launched in March 2010. In less than two years, the site was receiving more than 11 million visits each week, making it the fastest growing site in history.

You might think they were able to do this by spending millions in marketing, securing celebrity influencers, and turning popular pinners into their biggest marketers. In reality, they actively avoided all of this. In fact, they avoided practically every social networking and marketing "best practice" at the time. They didn't include any leaderboards, they didn't highlight the most popular pinners, they used an infinite scroll layout instead of pushing for more clicks and page views, and most interesting to me, their first community members weren't "influencers" with high Klout scores. They were *role models* who would care for the community as if it were their own.

From Fast Company (http://www.fastcodesign.com/1670681/ben-silbermann-pinterest):

In Pinterest's early days, Silbermann gave out his cell-phone number, attended blogger meet-ups, and personally composed weekly emails that were sent out to Pinterest's tiny, but growing, community. "It's like you've built this little city with nobody inside of it yet," he says. "And you want to fill it up with the right kinds of people who are going to teach future people what they should be doing when they move in." **Most Silicon Valley types look at early users as viral marketers; Silbermann saw them as role models.** *(Until recently, Pinterest's welcome email advised users to "pin carefully" because "your pins set the tone for the community." The site bans nudity and discourages users from posting images of too-skinny models, otherwise known as "thinspiration," after the phenomenon became a problem.)*

What if brands' PR and social media community managers stopped worrying about targeting the influencers with certain indicators:

- Most Klout (http://klout.com/home);

- Highest PeerIndex (http://www.peerindex.net/) score; or

- The highest Empire Avenue (http://empireavenue.com/) share price.

Instead, managers should worry about identifying the people who are best equipped to create and maintain a healthy community? What if we looked for qualities like good taste, helpfulness, and compassion instead of followers, page views, and likes? What if we focused our efforts on the people who will become the community leaders, rather than simply the people with the loudest mouths? If what we're doing is truly building online communities, shouldn't we first recruit the people who will actually be, you know, building that sense of community and modeling the behaviors you want to see from all members?

Now, if your goal is to simply get a million Facebook likes or sign up two million users to your branded community, then by all means, pay Lil Wayne to Tweet your URL to his 8 million followers and watch the numbers stack up. You can trot out your page views and member numbers to your boss all you want. Just don't expect those thousands of people to actually do what you want them to do.

On the other hand, if you're looking to build a vibrant community of brand advocates who will buy your products, share your messages with their networks, give you honest, constructive feedback and build other brand advocates, then you should instead look for people who will model those behaviors. These people may not have the biggest names or the most "influence," but they're the ones who will create the foundation for what your community will be.

THIS is the future of branding and community building – it's not about social or mobile or location aware apps or retargeting – it's about fundamentally rethinking what we learned about PR, advertising, creative, and digital in college. It's about making friends, and not Facebook friends or Twitter friends – it's about making real, honest-to-god *friends*. Friends who will forgive you when you mess up, who will accept a higher price because they understand and empathize with you, who will step up and defend you when you're being attacked, who will pay more because they share similar beliefs, and who will talk about you with their friends and family because they believe in you.

About the Author
Steve Radick is a vice president of public relations at Cramer-Krasselt, an integrated marketing and communications agency based in Chicago. He joined C-K in 2012 after more than eight years with government consulting firm, Booz Allen Hamilton, where he founded their digital strategy and social media practice. Steve has been an outspoken advocate of the role PR can and should play in brands' marketing efforts, especially when it comes to social media. He discusses his approach to PR and social media on his blog, "Social Media Strategery," located at www.steveradick.com and on Twitter at @sradick.

∞

Chapter 6: Brand Analysis

∞

Analyze Your Profile

This chapter is about brand analysis: assessing and evaluating you. Who does your community think you are? Are you effectively communicating what is important to you? Are you offering real value in the information you share with your communities of interest? Does the feedback you receive suggest you are offering value? Are the communities you seek accepting, or at least inquisitive about you and your information? These are the things we use for measurement and assessment. You can evaluate by traffic, feedback, requests for information, or any number of other things. But make sure you're asking the tough questions. The guidance in the branding chapter's challenge is relevant to this chapter as well. This is by no means easy, and Social Media 4EVR stresses that brand should be interwoven with end state and with the plan of action. Staying on message and on plan ensures brand durability, visibility, consistency, relevance, and a whole host of other considerations. When we brand, we are using a word or image to identify a person or organization or product; or all three. A brand separates us and helps people remember us. We need to analyze our success in reaching those we seek. Social networking success in branding comes when we develop effective analysis and measurement strategies. Don't just measure. If you find weaknesses or opportunities to improve, take the appropriate action.

∞

Once you've created that personal brand, make sure to keep tabs on its effectiveness. How do you do that? You can start by simply analyzing your participation. Are you answering questions on social media sites, and do you share links, videos or other content with your audiences? Do you post slide decks to sites like Slideshare? Do you upload advice or how-to videos, or do you write valuable content in a blog and answer resulting comments? Finally, do you invite, connect, link, etc., with people who share your interests?

These are all good questions to start with, but brand analysis is much more than asking questions. You need solid metrics to put your brand under the evaluation microscope. Keep an eye on your key metrics to see if they are growing and what behavior is influencing them. Determine the right level for your evaluation. For instance:

- **Followers, friends and subscriber counts**—The number of people you have following you is not the best metric, but it does tell you if you're attracting versus annoying people!

- **Retweets, clicks and shares**—If people want to share your stuff, it's a hint that what you are putting out is valuable.

- **Comments, favorites, discussions**—Can you spark discussion and debate? That's value right there.

You should also be true to the three Cs of personal branding: Clear, Consistent and Collaborative. Always be *clear* about who you are and who you are not and don't compromise that position for any reason. Be *consistent* in expressing your brand across all communication vehicles you employ. Take a *collaborative* approach to create regular, valuable content, because strong brands are always visible to their target audiences and invite feedback.

Building, managing and adjusting your personal brand are important to making your social media experience valuable. Managing your personal brand across all of your social media efforts can offer you an important place with your target audiences, but that's not the only benefit. An effectively managed personal brand can lead to connections, contacts or other interactions that may be useful to your life and your goals. Now, it may not be evident why you should interact with John or Jane Citizen when they first send you an invitation, but it's wise to think carefully before dismissing them.

It is helpful to look at invites as opportunities. You never know if the person you meet today will be important in the future. If you can cultivate that relationship right now, then you have a potential opening for later. Of course, not everyone in this world is honest or sincere or without bad intentions, but you might just take an optimistic view as you move through social networking. You can be successful by managing your profile and by not opening your whole life through social networking, posting just enough information to stay in touch with the digital conversation.

The bottom line is to be your own worst critic about your brand. Nurture it with attention and it will serve you well. Once you have good data from your brand analysis, you need to apply it to your social networking activities. You should work to generate excitement about you and your brand, or about your corporate brand. How do you do that? See Table 2 below.

Examining Branding

Table 2

Personal Brand Action	Motivation
▪ Accept the challenge of "owning the company."	▪ Yes, this is really about you!
▪ Determine your personal value and share that information in your engagements.	▪ This is no time to be shy!
▪ Celebrate your persona publicly.	▪ Remember that you seek attention and recognition!
▪ Evaluate yourself regularly.	▪ Test yourself on whether you're true to your persona.
▪ Strive to find your motivations.	▪ Use your interests, hobbies and adventures to make YOU irresistible!
▪ Establish a plan and follow it.	▪ Pursue challenging goals and objectives!
▪ Network, Network, Network.	▪ What more can be said about engaging?

Corporate Brand Action
Should be an easy adjustment from personal brand

- Accept the challenge of moving the company forward.
- Understand company values and share info in engagements.
- Accept your part in the organization.
- Assist in corporate evaluations as if you are the boss.
- Understand and follow the corporate plan.
- Network, Network, Network.

Barriers to Participation

To get ready for your engagement activities, you need to understand barriers to social networking participation, because they will be important to attracting and keeping partners in engagement. In your social networking efforts, you are working to establish attention and reputation that creates trust-based, lasting engagements. Knowing why people avoid or limit participation allows you to adjust the information you present and the ways in which you present it for maximum effectiveness.

These tips are intended to help organizations and individuals create social media policies and processes that assist with brand analysis. Getting involved in social media is easy. Evaluating the effectiveness of online interactions, providing security protections, analyzing return on investment, and understanding performance or participation implications can be daunting considerations.

Questions and concerns are inevitable based on the amount of time that is spent online. That's why it's important to evaluate participation as early and often as possible. If that doesn't happen as part of the goal-setting that should precede social networking "start-ups," it should happen as soon as possible and should be focused on a specified end state or goal.

There are many reasons that people do not participate in social networking. Well-publicized barriers to participation include fear, disbelief, underestimation of the benefits, lack of a sense of return on investment, misunderstanding of the capability, misperceptions about platforms, or a combination of all of these reasons.

Don't let the barriers stop you from engaging and participating fully. Build trust in your online interactions by assessing value-plus and value-minus exchanges. This can help you avoid situations where the risk in unacceptable for further participation. For those who are concerned about vulnerability to others, it is advisable to understand possible damage versus received advantage.

Evaluating the pros and cons of connecting will help you make good decisions on participation. Finally, be clear about your identity, be consistent in your engagements, and use a collaborative approach to build trust and social capital and reduce risk.

You can navigate any or all of these barriers with an open mind, an understanding of personal social media evolution, and keys to engagement.

Social Media Evolution

Social Media 4EVR is about establishing and articulating the why of social networking participation. Social networking does not have to be an all or nothing proposition. A look at the social media evolution in Table 3 is proof that one can tailor participation to personal likes and beliefs, allowing virtually anyone to get involved. On-line users go through normal, healthy stages.

There are some very specific actions you can take to make social networking very rewarding. Contribute content that is clear, concise and compelling. You can share things you find interesting or create original content. Take time to comment on what your target audience is saying, highlighting common interests along the way.

Using Safko's *Social Media Bible* and information from other social media experts leads us to some general categories of social media users. Table 3 can help with your participation.

Social Media Evolution

Table 3

User Stage	Characteristics
Visitors	Browse around to check people and places out.
Lurkers	Browse for weeks/months without announcing your presence.
Novices	Set up a presence and contribute content, such as comments.
Insiders	Start creating your own content to share with others.
Leaders	Become more experienced in terms of relationships and creating content.
Elders	Become expert in the particular aspect of social media, or at least continue to contribute.

Once you decide, take a formal approach to participation which consists of four actions: joining, listening, speaking and interacting. Join a community or engage with your stakeholders, using the basics of your personal profile to introduce yourself. Take time to listen to what they are saying and understand what the community of interest is about. Once you have a handle on what's going on, speak by letting the audience or community of interest know more about you. Begin sharing information and ideas with your new-found friends.

Getting involved in referrals is another great way to participate. Introduce people, refer friends to great deals, share information on forward-leaning companies you're involved in, or just communicate about what's going on in your community. Stay tuned in to whether you're reading or ignoring current communications. If you're not tuned in, you can't hear the digital conversation. If you don't have a social media goal, you might miss out on important communications because of the incredible speed at which the conversation moves. That speed increases every day, every hour, every minute.

Chapter 7: EVR: Analyzing Your Participation

∞

EVR

This chapter is about expectation, value and return (EVR). When Company A (name withheld) started with social media, the leadership was ecstatic that they were on the cutting edge. In growing the internal social media network and building community the company was very active, helping people build profiles, finding ways to take their profile photos at company events, conducting basic training on the platform, and creating "change champions" who sang the virtues of social media and continued to get people to sign up. There was a quota to meet in terms of how many people did the basics: post a photo, create a profile, and post one informational item. Once the company met the quota things slowed down. Finally, company leadership asked a question. "Since we've allowed everyone to use social media, are they performing any better, or are our profits increasing?" Turns out the team couldn't answer the question because beyond the participation quota, there was no end state determined at the beginning of the process. So the plan only got the team to a certain point, and it certainly didn't involve performance or profit measures. The bottom line is that you can't determine how to get to a destination if you don't know where you're going. The recurring theme here is let the destination, not the path, of social networking drive participation. To make that a reality, identify social media EVR. Identify the various roles in social media participation – visitor, lurker, novice, insider, leader, and elder – to find community members, participants and "change champions" to help you with social networking activities and progress. Finally, evaluate participation at every opportunity using your end state and your social media plan.

∞

Expectation, Value and Return, or EVR, is about using three keys to develop a winning social media plan that guides your activities in encouraging others to join your network. EVR is a partial response to the amount of negativity one encounters when talking to people about social media participation. While there can be many negative things about social media, the authors believe that the benefits far outweigh the problems.

Of course, people mention the value of staying in touch with family, friends and even colleagues. They also discuss joining groups that share your interests, your community, or your profession. But there are two things that people do not always consider as reasons to participate: (1) Help friends or potential employers find you, or (2) find a new job.

Many times, people just want to go on their way and be left alone. But the hardest time to find a person, or have a person find you, is when you really NEED it to happen. That may not happen very often with family and friends, but it is often the case with new employers and job searches. Some would say you have to look for your next job while you are still happy with your current job, and there's merit in that point of view. Keeping your profile alive as part of the digital conversation may prove helpful in ways you don't anticipate.

There is also a lot of "noise" in the channel, making it hard to find what's relevant. But connection brings the benefits of seeing and hearing current news and conversations. There is also a wealth of information and connections available that you cannot even imagine, so participating constantly gives you a chance to find out. You can easily filter or ignore anything that is not relevant for you.

So now we can discuss EVR, which is the key to social networking. This is how you demonstrate the WIIFM – what's in it for me – to your intended audience, whether they are one person or a group. In the true sense of social media interaction, people are motivated to contribute valuable information to a person or a group because of an expectation of value in return. We're talking about three things. First is the ability to get useful help in a two-way arrangement, and second is the opportunity for a valued information exchange. The third benefit to EVR is getting and giving recognition that matters to others.

Of course there's more to social media participation than just understanding EVR. But EVR gives you the tools to effectively connect with others.

© Can Stock Photo Inc./everythingpossible

Social Networking Filtering

Here's one approach to filtering connections. For LinkedIn and other sites, put connections in three categories: Acquaintances, Colleagues, and Partners. Acquaintances refers to everyone you accept, and you can further segment them into two groups: Testers and Prospects.

The Testers are people you are taking a chance on. With Testers, you probably don't have enough information to decide on whether to develop a networking relationship with them now, but there is a possibility that you will learn more later as they provide more background information. The Prospects are people who have given enough information to make a networking relationship decision. These are people whose profile is compelling and might be a fit for your social networking life.

Once you decide there's an opportunity to develop a networking relationship, you can move Acquaintances to Colleagues. Colleagues are people with whom you engage at every opportunity. You read their posts and like or comment as appropriate. You share content with them, especially when you blog. Get to know them better and let them get to know you better. There is no need to target specific activities to this group. Just communicate when it's convenient or when they reach out to you.

From the Colleagues, select a group of people to be Partners. These are people you want to include in your primary networking activities and communications. These are people whose profiles are most complementary to yours, or whose activities and interests are complementary to your social media and networking plans.

This group may only number 15-20 people at any given time; a number you can easily keep in touch with. Send them private messages and even conduct Skype video calls. To further illustrate the connection process, look at Malcolm Gladwell's *The Tipping Point* (2002). His book focuses on the kind of people who were included in Partners above. Gladwell makes the point that as a trend moves toward a tipping point, it is often shepherded to popularity by a small group of people classified as Connectors, Mavens and Salesmen.

Connectors are individuals who have ties in many different realms and act as conduits between them, helping to engender connections, relationships, and "cross-fertilization" that otherwise might not have ever occurred. **Mavens** are people who have a strong compulsion to help other consumers by helping them make informed decisions. They are the experts. **Salesmen** are people whose unusual charisma allows them to be extremely persuasive in inducing others' buying decisions and behaviors. Gladwell identifies a number of examples of past trends and events that hinged on the influence and involvement of Connectors, Mavens, and Salesmen at key moments in their development.

By segmenting connections into certain categories – Acquaintances, Colleagues and Partners – you can manage networks and relationships to your advantage. This is how you might make sense of social networking activity. It's also how you can protect your privacy and activity. It's an approach that can be helpful because some people may not understand social networking relationships, sometimes assuming that they have created a "real" relationship without cultivating the connection. Just because a person accepts a connection doesn't mean you've made a friend for life. Let's face it, some people have no social networking filter for friends or connections, accepting everyone without a thought. But it's important to understand the network relationship.

For instance, there are times when someone is accepted to connect, and they immediately ask the person to hire them, recommend them, introduce them to another connection, etc. Some might accept social media invitations to connect from people who don't have profile photos, even if they have a rule that they won't accept these people. One way to manage this is to send an e-mail asking how you know the person and whether they want to share some additional information. If they don't answer then there is no reason to connect. If they answer and you can make a good decision, you can accept them and use the approach below.

First, put new connections in an Acquaintances-Testers category. In this case, their status in networking is tentative at best. But be careful at the outset, because there are many instances when a new connection might ask you for a job or a recommendation as soon as you accept them. It might be best to ignore or disconnect these folks because those kinds of questions/favors are for cultivated relationships, where the person is a very special Colleague or a Partner. The point is, understand the relationship you've created and treat it with the proper connection behavior.

Acquaintances, Colleagues, Partners, Connectors, Mavens, Salesmen; it's the same train of thought. These considerations can help you build a trusted environment, brand yourself, and connect with your audience whether it's for a short-term or long-term. You could also use social networking to become a thought leader in your community if that's something you're interested in.

As you work through your connections, understand the importance of measuring those interactions. As you try to get better in your participation, you'll want to know how your actions are perceived by your audiences. You want to know when they are reading your posts so that you can post at the correct time on the best platform.

For organizations, return on investment (ROI) is the universal measure of success. Leaders will want to know ROI and employees will use ROI to demonstrate impact and effectiveness. You will be using a strategy and you need to have some indicators of cause and effect. Most important, the outcomes of your activities are crucial to decisions to determine next steps in your strategy or plan.

There are some very useful tools to help with measurement. Several of the best are listed in Table 4.

Social Media Measurement Tools

Table 4

Tool	Explanation
Hoot Suite	Dashboard to monitor and measure multiple social media platforms.
Google Analytics	Free resource to track and measure web sites and social media activities.
Radian6	Web-based service to track and measure an organization's social media strategy.
Moz Analytics	Tools to track and analyze an organization's social media and web presence.
Topsy	Track activity and influence on Twitter.

For more on how to be a connector, see Dennis Shiao's article at the end of this chapter.

Be Proactive

Now that you have some suggestions on connecting in social networking, it's time to focus on the dynamics of participation. A proactive approach on providing value in social networking offers great rewards. This book is all about having a plan, and being a connector is another great way to have meaning and purpose in your activities.

Many conversations about social networking start with people sharing information about the negatives that can be present in participation. However, there can be valuable interactions as long as you don't let social networking issues alone keep you from the gifts of interaction that are available. To accept those gifts, you simply need to realize the power of the online environment, accept the nature of unfettered communication, and get familiar with how to protect your privacy and the privacy of those in your network.

Realize the power of the online environment to help people create, share, adapt and reuse content to engage with others for meaningful dialogue and collaboration. Users can create linkages, groups and communities. Peer-to-peer contact facilitates meaningful social interaction, allowing people to create and maintain their own user profiles and IDs.

Remember unfettered communication? Your online content is discoverable, community moderated, persistent and subject to conditions of use. The conditions of use are set jointly by the community of interest or network and individual users.

Online platforms are public, so users should get familiar with privacy methods and settings to create "walls of immunity." Walls of immunity are each user's protection zone where they can dictate who knows what, when they know it, and whether they can interact or exchange information in the network or community involved. This ability is always available – 24/7 – from a range of devices and locations for the savvy communicator. Understanding how to protect privacy is important, especially when users are engaging a new or unknown audience.

Every day, we read about the problems of fraudulent interactions, spam and virus attacks, and identity theft. Negative comments about our public persona or about the information we post present a threat that many want to avoid at all costs. But don't let those negatives keep you from the benefits that social networking offers. Yes, there are perils out there, but there are safeguards available. For instance, identifying your audience, keeping a watch on privacy controls, managing your personal brand, and properly reviewing your posts for relevance, accuracy and propriety are ways to stay "safe."

The tactics mentioned above can protect you from threats and allow you to make course corrections when necessary. Most important, you're not alone in this; or you don't have to be. Every day, people around the globe try to make sense of social networking. They ask themselves any number of questions. Should I get involved? Should I be doing more? Am I using the right platform? Who should I be communicating with? Your network can help you cultivate an understanding of social media goals, roles and interactions.

Building Community

How does one's community really help? Here's a community of practice primer to help. This recipe for success starts with seven principles. According this approach, effectiveness relies on managing the "participation rule," facilitation needs and overall challenges. This is insightful for our examination of audience analysis and trust building. In "Cultivating

Communities of Practice," the Harvard Business School lists important considerations for building networks. They are:

- Design for evolution;
- Open a dialogue between inside and outside perspectives;
- Invite different levels of participation;
- Develop both public and private community spaces;
- Focus on value;
- Combine familiarity and excitement; and
- Create a rhythm for the community.

The principles suggest the best practices in creating and energizing a network of online partners that provide mutual benefits to all users. This kind of network features dynamic communication that continues despite changes in topics or tactics in the digital environment. This network allows anyone to participate in public and private interactions that are valuable to all. The resulting interactions tend to be cozy, exciting and easy for all community members to follow.

© Can Stock Photo Inc./daisydaisy

Effective use of the principles requires that participants first establish or identify a purpose and match that purpose with a relevant community of interest. Effective audience analysis at the beginning of this process means understanding the culture and behaviors of participants. This understanding allows development of the "practice," which means tools and techniques that are most conducive to interactions with the targeted audience. Finally, monitor and measure everything to ensure that the social communication fits the intent.

In 2006 authors and bloggers, Ben McConnell and Jackie Huba, coined the name "The 1% rule" for a theory about the way we interact online. The rule states that for every 100 people online, only 1 person will create content and 10 will "interact" with it. The other 89 will just view it. That means that anyone who creates content – you – is very important.

The next requirement is to facilitate, facilitate, facilitate. Do this by monitoring activity on a regular basis and encourage participation with a call to action in each post. To really keep up with managing the community, make an action plan complete with metrics and evaluations. Think about the meaning of online interactions and how they are affecting network participants, and ask questions to get others' views.

Many different players in the network have challenges that must be conquered to be successful. The management challenge is to focus on topics important to community members. Management must find a well-respected community member to coordinate things and must ensure people have time and encouragement to participate. Finally, it's necessary to build on the core values of the organization in online communications.

The challenge for the community is to get thought leaders involved to create interest and enthusiasm through interaction with subject matter experts. Community members need to cultivate personal relationships and need to find an actively passionate core group. Forums allow community members to think together and energize information sharing.

There are also technical challenges that, when conquered, make it easy to contribute and access the community's knowledge and practices. Finally, there are personal challenges to continuously create real dialogue about cutting-edge or high-entertainment issues.

The community of practice primer is a recipe for getting in touch and staying in touch through social networking partnerships. But we can do more to enhance our online communication activities.

Bonding, Bridging and Linking

Social capital can be characterized by bonding, bridging and linking. Bonding social capital is about establishing strong ties, which refer to connecting people in similar situations, such as immediate family, close friends and neighbors. Bridging social capital refers to establishing informal ties, connecting people with something in common and who are distant, like loose friendships and workmates. Linking social capital focuses on establishing voluntary ties, attracting "unlike people in dissimilar situations, such as those who are entirely outside of the community, thus enabling members to leverage a far wider range of resources than are available in the community (Woolcock and Narayan 2000)."

So what do we know about strength of ties? The strength of a tie is a combination of the amount of time, the emotional intensity, the intimacy and the reciprocal services that characterize the tie. Each tie is independent; however, they can be related based on social networking activities or other attempts to communicate. It is widely agreed that nearly all relationships – in person, online or otherwise created – start as weak ties and then have to develop into strong relationships. That development does not always happen, but it can and has been done. Weak ties are valuable because there is no requirement to develop them. But weak ties put you in touch with a greater audience than is available in anyone's network of strong ties. Then, in the audience analysis part of social networking, users can decide which weak ties deserve more development.

Strong ties are those family members or lifelong friends who are already in our inner circle, or close to it. The strong ties are the most valuable because they provide a starting point or, better yet, a community base for social networking activities. It is very easy to develop the larger network around these strong ties. Family notwithstanding, it takes a great deal of time to build strong ties, but when built they are irreplaceable.

Granovetter, in his strength of weak ties theory, argues that weak ties are valuable because similarity breeds liking, but that weak ties are local bridges (for connections). Some experts argue that networks with more weak ties have shorter paths, resulting in faster change and greater ability to coordinate (Borgatti 2000). What that means is that people get jobs from weak ties and large groups or organizations use weak ties to manage threats and opportunities. The Granovetter theory has developed into embeddedness, which states that all economic action, organizational and individual, is influenced and driven by social ties created and nurtured among individuals.

In a pure sense, strong ties facilitate access, allowing easier transfer of complex knowledge based on trust and familiarity with partners. Strong ties allow for social control, promoting the development of reputation and social capital in the form of trust and social norms. This is a view to great collaboration.

Weak ties, on the other hand, allow greater flexibility and access to new information and promote the transfer of simple knowledge. The value of weak ties lies in the great number of contacts available as well as in the diversity they bring to a network.

What does it all mean? It means that when people and organizations are analyzing audiences and deciding on growing communities, bonding, bridging, linking and ties will be involved whether people realize it or not. Understanding these constructs will be very beneficial to social networking adventures.

Perceived Improvement Potential

Author Michael Brown's research uses perceived improvement potential as one of the ways to measure social media effectiveness. Perceived improvement potential (PIP), then, clearly refers to the challenge of getting people to believe that an action will lead to improvement of their performance (Brown 2011). The challenge is twofold in this context. The first challenge involves understanding the dynamics of change processes. Management problems are created when people are reluctant to move from the status quo and accept new methods (Lasden 1981). If leadership takes the critical first step of developing understanding, they can address the four negative reactions to the introduction of a new system: sense of awkwardness, fear and suspicion, misunderstanding and resentment (Lasden 1981). The keys to success involve improving participation through education and information programs, and beginning the change with mild participatory measures and then moving to tactics that are more forceful.

The second challenge involves addressing an individual's determination of whether the change will result in some level of performance improvement. For instance, a study conducted among 100 international senior executives involved in technological innovation within their firms examined barriers to in-house diffusion of new ideas (Vandermerwe 1987). First among the barriers listed was the difficulty of making observable benefits clear to others. It is equally important to examine different forms of technological change resistance in this study. In one study, Kulmann (1988) summarized research findings about new product adoption, human stress and resistance to technological change. That summary lists five items:

- Technical change is resisted only when employees perceive the change as a threat to their interests.

- Employees will strongly support an innovation if they are confident in their prediction of the consequences that the change will have upon them.

- The innovation will be better accepted if employees believe they have control over the changing situation.

- The change will be accepted to the degree that those concerned perceive no hindrance to their established working habits and values.

- Support for the innovation will increase if employees are given an opportunity to utilize it on a step-by-step basis.

Marsh (1990) argued that accepting change boils down to being open-minded, explaining that people generally have fatal failings when it comes to embracing new ideas and making them work. One of the failings is especially relevant: people don't really believe the idea will work. This is why PIP is so important, because it involves a conscious determination of whether the activity or commitment involved will bring personal benefits. Social learning (Bandura 1977) suggests the need for concrete incentives to participate in the kind of social networking that an organization values.

The key to PIP, then, is all about breaking down barriers. Dr. Tudor Rickards, an English consultant in creative problem solving, has identified four groups of barriers to change, or blocks: strategic, value, perceptual and self-image (Marsh 1990). Strategic blocks deal with the way we implement ideas and are influenced by previous experience and habit. Value blocks deal with our approach to ideas, which are influenced by our prejudices, traditions and upbringing. Perceptual blocks deal with task orientation and are influenced by our single-mindedness or what we are doing at the time ideas are presented, especially if we are pressed for time or under stress. Self-image blocks deal with whether people believe they have the ability to implement new ideas and are influenced by experience and the reactions of others. Understanding these barriers, and adjusting to them, is important to, as Marsh (1990) says, "meeting the challenge of change."

That's really what our social networking journey is all about, "meeting the challenge of change" and making it count for your best interests. Yes, there are perils along the way, giving us many reasons to avoid social networking. This book attempts to address the various reasons that outweigh the perils and offer great reasons to participate. You just need a little time and an open mind. The current advances in technology applications put you in charge of your security, so take a chance!

∞

How to Be a Connector on Social Networks
By Dennis Shiao

In his book "The Tipping Point," author Malcolm Gladwell describes the role of The Connector. Gladwell profiles the country's most famous Connector, Paul Revere. Revere's "British are coming!" horse ride played a critical role in The American Revolution. It took a Connector like Revere to awaken the countryside and spur the revolutionaries into action.

Fast forward to 2010 and there were Connectors who played key roles in the Arab Spring revolutions. This time, the Connectors used online social networks as a key vehicle for communications. While your own objectives with social media may not reach the level of overthrowing a government, you can accrue tremendous value by becoming a Connector. Let's consider five ways to become a Connector on social networks.

1. Share liberally.

Whether it's Twitter, Facebook or Pinterest, share often. Curate carefully, then share liberally. Don't share for the sake of sharing, share interesting and useful content. As you share, you'll gain a following. The size of your following is important, but even more important is their "quality" – that is, the likelihood that they take action based on what you share.

2. Reciprocate generously.

To become a Connector, give back as much (or more) as you receive. On Twitter, follow back "real people," while avoiding the spam bots. Celebrities may have a 10x or 100x ratio on followers to following, but Connectors are closer to 1:1. In other words, if you're not "following your followers," you'll find it hard to attain Connector status.

3. Really get to know people.

I've had the privilege of meeting great people on social networks and developing meaningful relationships with them. I'd love to meet them in person someday, but realize that some I never will. But that doesn't stop me from getting to know them deeply, via their tweets, posts and status updates. Connectors can "connect" most effectively when they truly know the people on either side of the connection.

4. Give without expecting anything in return.

Some people give with the explicit thought that they'll get something in return later. Connectors give freely, without any consideration for quid pro quo. After all, if you're constantly wondering about when you'll be "paid back," you're too busy to facilitate or perform the key tasks of a Connector.

5. Facilitate introductions and nurture relationships.

Think of Connectors as online matchmakers. Sure, sometimes they'll introduce two people romantically. Other times, they'll facilitate business relationships or partnerships. Or, they may simply introduce people who'd find each other's thoughts fascinating.

Online social networks make it quite convenient for aspiring Connectors. As a first step, identify existing Connectors that you're following. Observe their actions, so that you can model their behaviors. Once you have a solid foundation of understanding, begin the sharing process. That will lead to developing a following, which will lead to opportunities to facilitate connections.

About the Author

Dennis is director of product marketing at INXPO and author of the book "Generate Sales Leads With Virtual Events." At INXPO, Dennis is responsible for go-to-market strategy and execution, and for shaping product and platform evolution via the "voice of the customer." Dennis has managed virtual event campaigns for Cisco, HP, Oracle and Microsoft, among others. Dennis blogs about virtual events at INXPO, and on his personal blog, "It's All Virtual." Dennis can be found on Twitter at @dshiao.

∞

Chapter 8: Planning and Policy Implications

∞

Establish A Road Map For Your Actions

This chapter is about planning and policy. They go hand in hand. Before you determine your plan, it is important to have some policies. Policies are principles, rules and guidelines that are used to reach long-term goals. They are part of your, or your organization's, culture, and they are widely accessible. Policies influence major decisions and actions and provide boundaries within which activities are conducted. Policies translate into steps, using a plan, that result in an outcome compatible with personal and professional viewpoints. You should set a plan that is a detailed roadmap for goals, objectives and tactics. Review the plan at regular points to ensure it covers all the necessary activities for success. Stay on the path of the plan to ensure you are moving to the desired end state. A carpenter might say, "Measure twice, cut once." That means take extra time and care to evaluate the actions required, maybe taking a break and then reviewing again. Once you start to take the necessary actions set out by the plan, follow proper procedures. Finally, develop a social media plan that addresses goals in support of your personal and professional brand.

∞

Social media – be it services like Facebook, Twitter and BlogSpot, or comment/share functions via traditional media – is a means to paint a picture about who you are and what you believe in. It's a public billboard – free advertising – a shout or whimper seen by anyone and everyone you determine. Even with the use of privacy settings so only your friends or followers can view your online journal, you are broadcasting your ideas to a wide network. Thus it's important to remember that when crafting your personal brand online, your story telling should be done with care and attention and an understanding that this watercolor may also connect to the professional brand.

This chapter looks at the corporate perspective in managing a social workforce and how individual behavior affects corporate reputation. With one billion Facebook users, 400 million Google+ accounts, 7 billion Flickr photos, Twitter, Tumblr, Pinterest, FourSquare and others... it may seem fruitless to create a corporate social media policy that seeks to influence individual behavior online. However, the breadth of the social media universe requires that companies develop policy managing this intersection of corporate reputation and the personal brand of employees.

Let's start with thoughts about the community in which you participate. In other words, what's your current environment? You will have to get in touch with your community either as the manager or as a leading participant.

While a corporate social media policy can also address how the company will moderate comments and its expectations of customer engagement online, this chapter addresses only the employee engagement aspect.

When you set out to develop – or interpret and follow – an institutional social media policy, two considerations are paramount. First, don't be a puppet master. An organization cannot control individual communications, but you can set values and expectations. Second, involve all corporate functions in the development of the policy. The authors of this book hope that the public relations executives and team are leading the process. Yet, legal, IT, human resources, finance, marketing, operations and representatives from general staff to the executive office will play an important role in forming, teaching and implementing the policy. In fact, human resources is typically responsible for enforcing social media policies.

When forming the policy team, you will want to select a cross section of individuals from throughout the organization – senior management and mid-level and junior staff. This will help ensure that the policy is informed by different experiences and engagement with social media. Senior management, for example, is not likely being comprised of a majority of digital natives, whereas younger staff has most likely grown up in the digital age. Each brings an important perspective to the development process.

Also, that team needs to work as a unit, providing a commonality of effort. Leadership is key here, and there are any number of ways to keep the effort on track, such as setting up a working group that owns the task, setting milestones that are visible throughout the organization's activities, employing a community manager to keep you on track, or focusing on and emulating best practices.

For more on community managers, see Jason Mollica's article at the end of this chapter.

Best Practices

If best practices are the way you want to go, select your policy team and dive in. Let's go over some best practices to follow in the creation of or the revision of corporate social media policy. Keys include:

- Setting policy that coincides with corporate values and culture;
- Be positive;
- Be practical;
- Be transparent;
- Identify consequences;
- Make your policy easy to find;
- Teach your policy at every opportunity; and
- Keep your policy current.

1. To begin, set policy consistent with corporate values and culture. Review your company's mission statement and strategic plan as the first step to align social media policy with organizational culture. Also, ensure that the social media policy is consistent with other organizational policies, such as those for company-provided mobile devices or records retention.

Much has been written about the Coca-Cola Company's social media policy, in large part because it is a good model for how corporate values inform policy and guidance to employees for behavior online. It begins with Coca-Cola's shared organization values – leadership, collaboration, integrity, accountability, passion, diversity, and quality – that in turn inform its online social media principles. The policy makes it clear that all employees, whether a designated online spokesperson or an employee operating as an individual, act as ambassadors of the Coca-Cola brand. You can view the policy at: http://www.coca-colacompany.com/stories/online-social-media-principles/.

2. Be positive in the tone of your policy. Explain what employees can DO versus what you DON'T want them to do. Employees are online, so acknowledge that fact and treat employees as responsible guardians of both personal and corporate brands.

Be practical in spelling out how this tool can be used. Develop a short and easy to monitor and follow social media policy rather than a multi-page treatise. This also means that the policy should treat social media and online behavior generally, not channel by channel.

Many news organizations, for instance, encourage reporters to have an online presence on Twitter, and many also use Facebook and other channels to advance their professional brand online – one that can sometimes easily blur with a personal brand. In July 2011 (then November 2011 and then again in January 2012) the Associated Press updated its social media policy focused on Twitter and Facebook because it did not want its reporters breaking news first on Twitter or to give the appearance of being too cozy with sources who may also be followers or friends online. The AP received significant negative publicity for the perception that they were micromanaging online behavior. The AP missed an opportunity to incorporate these new media platforms into its reporting philosophy.

3. Be transparent in how you apply the policy. Clarify individual responsibility and how employees should identify with the corporate brand online. Many companies ask staff to add a disclaimer to personal accounts like "these views are my own." This is useful especially if an employee plays a role in the corporate online branding and needs some distinction between business and personal accounts.

4. Identify consequences of violations. As mentioned above, even with "privacy" settings, participating on social media is a very public activity. Therefore, it is important to restate that corporate confidentiality policies apply to information shared online. That way everyone knows what is expected and what happens when those expectations are not met.

Also, state what action could be sought to redress reputational damage occurring from individual online activity. From an employee who shares confidential information online to one who posts questionable photos or comments about being intoxicated, everyone should know that problem behavior could lead to termination.

5. Your policy must be easy to find for everyone, regardless of their level of participation in company social media activities. Post the corporate social media policy on the public institutional website. Customers and employees should know rules of engagement. Placement on the intranet can address apathy.

6. Teach policy; don't just distribute written copy. Make yours a living document that everyone can understand. This can be accomplished through an online tutorial or face-to-face sessions led by respected staff (e.g. someone perceived as a colleague) depending on the size of your organization. This instruction should include hypothetical examples of the policy in action. When employees are engaged in understanding policy, they are more likely to follow it.

7. Be sure to update your policy regularly. Given the rapid evolution of social media channels, review your corporate policy every six months, if not quarterly. You may determine no changes are needed. However, it's important to continue to verify facts and processes to stay current.

As you embark on developing a corporate social media policy, these principles will help guide you and the team in preparing and implementing the policy. It's also helpful to study what other institutions have done. From global companies – the International Olympic Committee, Southwest, Best Buy or Coca-Cola – to peer institutions, you can learn from the experiences of others.

With social media, the intersection of personal and corporate brand may seem complex; and it is. However, crafting a corporate social media policy is a critical tool to navigate these territories. The guidelines presented here are a foundation upon which you can explore and craft your own institutional policy.

Intel Social Media Guidelines

These are the official guidelines for social media at Intel. If you're an Intel employee or contractor creating or contributing to blogs, wikis, social networks, virtual worlds, or any other kind of social media both on and off intel.com—these guidelines are for you. We expect all who participate in social media on behalf of Intel to be trained, to understand and to follow these guidelines. Failure to do so could put your future participation at risk. These guidelines will continually evolve as new technologies and social networking tools emerge—so check back once in awhile to make sure you're up to date.

When You Engage

Emerging platforms for online collaboration are fundamentally changing the way we work, offering new ways to engage with customers, colleagues, and the world at large. It's a new model for interaction and we believe social computing can help you to build stronger, more successful business relationships. And it's a way for you to take part in global conversations related to the work we are doing at Intel and the things we care about. If you participate in social media, please follow these guiding principles:

1. Stick to your area of expertise and provide unique, individual perspectives on what's going on at Intel and in the world.
2. Post meaningful, respectful comments—in other words, no spam and no remarks that are off-topic or offensive.
3. Always pause and think before posting. That said, reply to comments in a timely manner, when a response is appropriate.
4. Respect proprietary information and content, and confidentiality.
5. When disagreeing with others' opinions, keep it appropriate and polite.
6. Know and follow the Intel Code of Conduct and the Intel Privacy Policy.

Full policy at: http://www.intel.com/sites/sitewide/en_SA/social-media.htm/.

∞

5 Ways You Can Be an Effective Community Manager
By Jason Mollica

Let's be honest... the title of Community Manager comes with great responsibility. You represent the online "voice" for a company or brand. One wrong Facebook post or Tweet and it could mean embarrassment (see Link 1 at end) for a brand or disaster for an individual (see Link 2 at end).

Managing a number of Facebook and Twitter accounts requires you to be on top of your game and on the lookout for positive and negative responses. It's also necessary to make sure a solid posting plan is in place prior to any engagement.

With that said, here are five steps that can really assist you and/or your brand in being an effective community manager.

Understand Your Audience: If you think that because you've managed a retail client it means that you understand a healthcare client, think again. These are two different audiences. Research and ask questions to see how they want to be represented. Also, look at competitors to see what they are doing. No competitors? You have a chance to stand out then.

Create a Posting Plan: Can't be stressed enough. If you are Tweeting and posting on Facebook without a content plan, you will get burned. While you may post something that is off the plan, it is absolutely integral that you have this "map." The plan keeps you focused and on message.

Short and Sweet: Twitter allows for 140 characters, but don't use all of them. Allow room for a retweeted comment or hashtags. On Facebook, just because you have more allocated space, doesn't mean you should write a book. Make your message effective, sharable, and, most importantly, memorable. That said...

Stay Away from All Caps and Too Many Exclamation Points: While they may draw attention to you, it's not for the right reasons. All caps posts show you are doing the virtual waving of hands, saying, "Look at me!" A number of sports teams and TV networks use this practice. The combination of "LIKE THIS" with multiple exclamation points isn't an effective post or strategy. It just shows you are begging for likes.

Be Honest: This should be a no-brainer. You can't make things up as a brand/individual. Followers WILL see through this. The more honest and transparent you are, the better you will be if/when something negative happens. People are apt to forgive you if you've been honest with them.

There are certainly other things to add to this list, but the 5 listed above should give you a good guide to community management. You may already be managing a small brand or a large company's social networks. Take a look at your own posting and see if you have put the top five to use. It could help and enhance your social appearance.

About the author

Jason Mollica is the president of *JRM Comm*, a public relations and social media marketing consultancy. He specializes in analyzing how social media and PR 2.0 impact today's changing landscape. A former television and radio producer, Jason also provides media training and social media training camps to Fortune 500 companies and various sized businesses around the country. He can be found on Twitter, @JasMollica, his blog, One Guy's Journey, website JRMComms.com, as well as YouTube and Facebook.

Link 1:
http://www.cnbc.com/id/47704401/Starbucks_Irks_the_Irish_by_Calling_Them_British

Link 2: http://usatoday30.usatoday.com/news/washington/2011-06-06-Anthony-weiner-sexting-twitter_n.htm

NOTE: This guest post is from PR 2.0 Strategies. Please meet the blog's author.

About the author

Deirdre Breakenridge has been in PR and marketing for 20 years helping senior executives in mid-size to large organizations communicate to their stakeholders. She is a PR strategist who has on many different types of communications programs, including thought leadership, image and reputation management, crisis communications, media relations, PR 2.0 and social media programs.

∞

Chapter 9: Designing a Social Media Plan

∞

Scheduling Activity and Measuring Success

This chapter is about social media planning. Social Media 4EVR teaches that anything in social media worth doing needs a good plan to be successful. If you fail to plan, then you plan fail. Planning is about setting goals, developing strategies and outlining tasks and schedules to get to an end state. The plan helps with the necessary objectives that can help to clarify, focus and research what is needed for successful participation. The plan also provides a logical framework within which the social media endeavor can exist and prosper, and it provides a benchmark against which actual social media participation can be measured and reviewed. There you have it; a system of checks and balances! The plan helps with assessing the effectiveness of social networking activities.

∞

When you think about social networking, you should think about expectation, value and return, or EVR. EVR is about using three keys to develop a winning social media plan that defines your participation and encourages others to join your network. While there can be many negative things about social networking, we believe that the benefits far outweigh the problems.

Of course, people mention the value of staying in touch with family, friends and even colleagues when they talk about social media. They also discuss joining groups that share their interests, their community, or their profession. But there are two things that people may not consider as valid reasons to participate: help friends or potential employers find them, or find a new job. And one more thing, how about the chance to explore exciting new people and places?

Given those suggestions, an active profile and participation in the digital conversation on a regular basis may prove beneficial. In the process, there may be unexpected value found in ways and places that don't seem obvious. Also, there is a lot of "noise" in the channel, making it hard to find what's relevant. Connection can bring the benefits of seeing and hearing current news and conversations. There is a wealth of information and engagements available that you cannot even imagine, so participating constantly gives you a chance to find out. You can easily filter or ignore anything that is not relevant for you.

So EVR is the key to social networking participation where we can find value through three things. First, get useful help in a two-way arrangement. Second, seize the opportunity for a valued information exchange. The third benefit is exchanging recognition that matters to others. These considerations can help you build a trusted environment, brand yourself, and connect with great people.

Again, there are many reasons to avoid social networking; however, there are even more reasons for involvement. Take some time, open your mind, and see how current advances in online communications put you in charge of your security. Take a chance!

Let's Talk Planning

From Lady Gaga to the London or Sochi Olympics; from the US Airways crash into the Hudson River to the Arab Spring social uprising; there are numerous examples of social media success stories. And several well-publicized "tweets heard round the world" that perhaps the author wished he'd kept private; former Congressman Anthony Weiner's sexting is but one illustration.

Some successes are well-planned strategies to build a personal or corporate brand. Some, like Occupy Wall Street and Arab Spring, are movements that utilized social media to mobilize activists and share information. Others are short-lived explosions – postings that yield unintended consequences.

The rest of this chapter seeks to inform a strategic approach to social media planning. With research and clearly defined goals and audiences, you can create a plan that will deliver results. But it all begins with "why" you want to engage on social media. Corporations often want to be visible online to promote a service or product. For individuals, the desire could be to position yourself as a subject matter expert (aka thought leader). Both activities help build and reinforce branding. The key to successful social media strategies in both instances is engagement with your target audience. Are you connecting and collaborating or simply pushing content?

Therefore, know what you want to say and to whom you want to talk. From there, you can determine on what channels you want to share and how often. Let's begin reinforcing the essential principles of social media, which include accessibility, smart choices, simplicity, authenticity, and good timing.

Accessibility means that anyone can be a publisher. That's why you should make your words show impact. As you write, choose your platforms wisely. No one can be everywhere online at once. Know where your audience will be and establish your presence there.

Simplicity is memorable. Twitter forces you to be brief, but don't sacrifice your story to that limitation. Write meaningful observations to establish your relevance and attract followers. Authenticity is essential, so be honest, truthful and accessible/responsive. Be real. Show your personality. Even if you tweet about industry trends, it's okay to share personal information occasionally too.

Finally, timing matters. From time of day to day of the week, when you post affects your visibility. Match your activity with the "calendar" to get the most bang for your buck.

Beginning any plan starts with knowing (1) what you want to say; (2) to whom; and (3) where you will connect with your audience. First, the hallmark of good public relations is storytelling. Social media has amplified the opportunities for storytelling. A well-crafted story helps you establish credibility and relevance – thus building social capital and influence.

> "Marketing [PR] is storytelling, but not in a pitch 'Look at me' way. If you're real and honest, people are going to know it." CC Chapman, author, Amazing Things Will Happen (via Vocus Demand Success 2013).

Second, define your audience. Are they peers, customers, or influencers themselves?

Third, where is your audience? Know what social media platforms they use and then select wisely. The better known social media channels include:

- Facebook – The most pervasive social media channel used mostly for sharing personal information.
- Twitter – While this is a smaller user base than Facebook, a platform used by influencers and reporters.
- Google+ – While not as ubiquitous Facebook, Google+ Hangouts are growing in popularity.
- LinkedIn – Professional channel to highlight your subject matter expertise and collaborate with industry peers.
- Tumblr – One of most popular blogging platforms.
- YouTube or Instagram or Flickr – Photos and videos convey messages concisely and have potential to become viral sensations.

> "I think [Twitter is] a PR medium. Again, it's very effective word-of-mouth. If you look at the Olympics in London, the big winner was Twitter. It wasn't Facebook. It wasn't even Google. We see analysis of the Twitter feeds every day, and it's very, very potent. But – and this is the old fart speaking – I think because it's limited in terms of number of characters, it reduces communications to superficialities and lacks depth." Sir Martin Sorrell, CEO of WPP Group, in an interview the *Harvard Business Review* on March 1.

So, plan your work; work your plan. For more on planning, see Diane Jones' article at the end of this chapter.

Now, you should be ready to do some planning for your social networking activities. The following pages give you some hands-on examples to work through end state (Table 5), use a social media plan template, and examine a sample social media plan.

The Social Networking Journey

Table 5

End State	Planning Focus
Help friends or potential employers find you Find a new job	Seek commonality: import e-mail address book, search profiles, seek friends of friends, or take advantage of people search engines in various platforms.
Increase connections	Conduct audience analysis: figure out who uses, or should use, your website, what information they need, and which tasks they must complete.
Connect with employees	Conduct online review: check sites like Facebook, LinkedIn and Twitter to get a sense of who they are.
Become a thought leader in your field	Find your niche: conduct keyword matching of online activities.
Find a thought leader	Environment scanning: find out who's leading the conversation about your topic and who others are recommending as great speakers.
Interaction	Conduct community building: listen to communities interact, join those that peak your interest and, then get engaged.
Feedback or decision making	Reach out: use the benefits of blogs, chats and webinars to seek conversations.
Marketing	Get active: use the benefits of speed to build social capital and exchange value.
Employee and/or leader development	Get connected: use EVR and emotional intelligence as a great start to connect in two-way communications that are beneficial to maximum performance.

SAMPLE TEMPLATE

1. Introduction: Explain your plan.

2. Objectives

    a. Increase number of visitors to my website by 10% in 6 months

    b. Improve my online presence by creating about 2 audience responses per week in 3 months

    c. Increase my posting and blogging by 20% in the next 2 months

3. Audience

4. Communication Strategy *(Based on the 4 pillars)*

    a. Approach *(Communicate, Collaborate, Educate, Entertain)*

    b. End State

5. Key Success Factors

    a. Direct access to your community of interest

    b. Ability to show value in what your provide

    c. Ability to discuss the benefits of continued interaction

    d. Opportunity to use a "push" approach to create a "pull" approach, in other words, start by reaching to them, and then show the value of *THEM* reaching to *YOU!*

6. Measurement

7. Content Development and Distribution

8. Benefits

Social Media Plan Components

1. **Introduction:** This should outline the challenge or opportunity that is motivating your social media participation. Why are you participating in social media and who is your audience?

2. **Goals:** These are general guidelines that explain what you want to achieve in your social media participation. They can be short- or long-term and represent overarching visions such as "promote myself as a leader in my field." Examples of your social media goals could be:

   a. Drive traffic to my website;

   b. Increase my connections or followers; or

   c. Establish myself as a thought leader in my community

3. **Objectives:** These declarative statements help define the strategy and implementation steps to attain the goals. Unlike goals, objectives are "SMT" – specific, measurable and time-bound with a completion date. They outline the "who, what, when, where and how" of reaching the goals. Establishing your objectives is often the most challenging part of creating the plan. Examples of your social media objectives could be:

   a. Increase the number of visitors to my website by 10 percent within 6 months;

   b. Improve my online presence by generating an average of 2 follower responses per week in 3 months; or

   c. Increase my posting and blogging by 20 percent in the next 2 months.

4. **Audience:** Defining your audience is as critical as clarifying your objectives. If you aren't talking to someone who's interested in you and your subject matter, you might as well have a Google+ Hangouts with the wall. Clearly define *who* you are trying to engage and outline their social profile. If it's a business audience, they might be more likely to be on LinkedIn, Twitter and blogs than Facebook, Pinterest or Foursquare. If you have time and resources, conducting research on your audience to identify their interests and social media habits is extremely useful to targeting and segmenting.

5. **Communication Strategy** (Based on the 4 pillars): What pathway will you take to make the kinds of connections that will impact audiences and achieve objectives?

    a. Approach (Communicate, Collaborate, Educate, Entertain).

    b. End State: What outcomes do you expect from your participation? For instance, do you want to grow business, increase your network, or find help with a problem? These would be end states.

6. **Channels:** Choose your social media channels and platforms wisely. Select 1 or 2, maybe 3 that will connect you with your target audience. It's unlikely they are actively engaging multiple channels, so why should you try to be everywhere at once? Consider whether Facebook, Twitter, LinkedIn, Google+, Tumblr, YouTube, Instagram or Flickr would be most appropriate.

7. **Tone/Voice:** What is the tone you want to set? Whatever you choose, it should be an authentic representation of you or your organization.

8. **Tactics – Content Development and Distribution:** What topics will you discuss? What type of content will you share? What percentage will be original vs. shared articles, photos, infographics? How much personal vs. professional information will you post?

9. **Timing:** What is the frequency of your postings? What time of day and week are most likely to garner attention?

10. **Key Success Factors:**
    a. Direct access to your community of interest.
    b. Ability to show value in what you provide.
    c. Ability to discuss the benefits of continued interaction.
    d. Opportunity to use a "push" approach to create a "pull" approach, in other words, start by reaching to them, and then show the value of *THEM* reaching to *YOU!*

11. **Measurement:** If you don't take time to evaluate your plan, you won't know what's working and what needs fixing or adjusting. There are several free tools, such as Google Analytics, Hoot Suite and Twitter Reach, to help you track your accomplishments.

Following this outline will help you set realistic goals and objectives to measure success. Most of us will never achieve the notoriety of Lady Gaga online. However, planning your social media strategy is time well invested.

Now, you're armed with information to help you get started with a draft plan that you might use as a "plug and play" device. Start by asking yourself, what are the compelling considerations?

- Objective – what are we trying to accomplish with our social media presence? This must come first and can often be much more difficult to discern than one might surmise.

- Audience – who are we trying to engage and what do we know about their social profile? Audience segmentation is often required and can result in multiple strategic pathways.

- Communication Strategy and Tactics – what pathway will we take to make the kinds of connections that will impact our audiences and achieve our objectives?

- Measurement – social media is an analyst's dream providing enormous amounts of data. Which metrics are most important? Why? Which actions lead to the desired outcome and how can they be measured?

- Content Development and Distribution – what are we going to say, do or proclaim? How often and where? Which platforms make the most sense and why?

Using Facebook Ads to Spread the Word...Quickly
By Diane W. Jones, MPA, APR

In November 2012, a one-cent sales tax was up for renewal in Pasco County, Florida. The "Penny for Pasco" had been in effect for nearly 10 years and had paid for numerous important projects, from building new schools and fire stations, to purchasing environmentally sensitive lands and new police cars.

Even though the Penny for Pasco had done so many good things for Pasco County over the last 10 years, its passage was far from guaranteed. Anything with the word "tax" associated with it had an uphill battle that election year. What made things even more difficult was the placement of the Penny for Pasco on the ballot – dead last, on the back of the ballot!

Because neither the county government nor the school board could legally campaign for an issue, a Political Action Committee (PAC) was formed to campaign for the renewal of the Penny for Pasco. In addition to the basic activities that take place during any campaign (fundraising, direct mail pieces, media relations, website, and Speaker's Bureau presentations) the PAC also introduced a Facebook page and Twitter account. Of the two, it quickly became obvious that our target audience was more likely to be on Facebook than Twitter, so we focused our attentions there.

Initially, we relied on organic growth for our Facebook page, using new posts and the hope of people sharing our information to increase Likes. This worked, but very slowly, with only a few new Likes each day. Because we had a very strict deadline for our campaign – Election Day – we needed as many people to see and Like our Facebook page as quickly as possible. So, we decided to use Facebook Ads.

We began the campaign on October 11, 2012, at which time we had 59 Likes. On Election Day, less than one month later, we had over 2,700 who had Liked our page and were following us. Those followers had shared our information to tens of thousands of other Facebook users, hopefully some of which were Pasco County voters.

The Penny for Pasco passed almost 70 percent, which is unheard of for a tax in these tough economic times. While we will never know what percentage of those voters said "Yes" to the Penny because of what they read on Facebook, we are confident that this social network played a part in our success.

For this campaign, Facebook Ads were a good choice because it allowed us to reach a large number of people quickly for very few dollars. However, while we were able to target ads based on geographic region, we were not able to target likely voters only, which is a drawback to Facebook Ads.

Overall, Facebook Ads are a very effective marketing tool for projects or campaigns that need to reach a large audience in a short time, with a very short and simple message. Our "Vote Yes" message fit that bill perfectly.

About the Author
Diane W. Jones, MPA, APR, is the president of DJ Public Relations, a boutique public relations agency that specializes in helping any size business or organization communicate with various publics that impact their bottom line. This is done through a variety of PR strategies, from online marketing and social media to media relations and community engagement. Diane is a member of the Public Relations Society of America (PRSA) having served as president of her local Tampa Bay PRSA chapter; chair of the Sunshine District, which encompasses the entire state of Florida; and chair of the PRSA District Council, which oversees PRSA districts throughout the country.

∞

Chapter 10: Crisis Communication

∞

Communicating At Light Speed

This chapter is about crisis communication, which deals with emergencies or surprise situations that can affect personal or professional livelihood, reputation and/or culture. Crisis communication is part of public relations practice and requires that one try to mitigate damage or other negative effects of a situation. Success is based on getting the attention of the public with factual information and positive communications. These are serious situations, and the public wants to know what you did, why you did it, and what you're trying to do next. The relationship of crisis communications to social media is about speed. News travels at light speed, and you often must try to match that speed when mitigating the situation and delivering messages that matter. Our challenge is to assess the effectiveness of social media in crisis situations.

∞

NOTE: This chapter features a series of endnotes to give readers relevant URLs for the text presented.

Social media, reputation management and crisis response are a perfect storm. In an age of TV anywhere and social media everywhere, the potential for a crisis situation is high. The general consensus on crisis communications is that an individual or institution has 15 to 60 minutes to respond to a crisis from the time it begins – not from the time it is discovered by the official responder. The first hour to 48 hours are typically the most critical time as a crisis unfolds. Most crises will fade from the focus of mainstream media within 72 hours if there isn't new information to drive the story forward.

The fast-paced nature of crises requires the ever-increasing speed of communication available through social media. Bloggers and other concerned citizens in an increasing number of instances are the first to report the news, and social media engages both individuals and organizations in "breaking news." Social media provides an opportunity to share messaging without the filter of traditional media, but intensifies the dynamic of immediacy because waiting to craft a response is no longer an option.

Therefore, prepare for possible crisis situations by taking into account the following considerations:

1. What social media channels are necessary for your response?

2. Who is the key spokesperson?

3. What type of messaging will help clarify the situation and the individual's or organization's role in it?

4. How can the individual or organization rebuild the public's trust?

The probability that a corporate or personal crisis will begin, or at least be magnified, online and via social media channels is increasingly likely. This chapter seeks to outline the characteristics of a crisis on social media and offer a few tips for reputation management.

Corporate and Celebrity Crisis

In 2010, it was hard to escape the Deepwater Horizon oil spill, better known as the BP oil spill, in the Gulf of Mexico on April 20. BP had spent years and millions of dollars creating a brand where British Petroleum became Beyond Petroleum. Within 24 hours of the spill, BP became synonymous with Big Pollution. Within a week, a fake Twitter account, @BPGlobalPR, had twice as many followers as the official corporate Twitter account. Within two weeks, a sea turtle was found dead and other oil-soaked animals washed on shore and oil flooded the coast within a month. With oil still spewing from the pipeline, CEO Tony Hayward famously quipped: "I'd like my life back." Congress investigated. BP created a $20 billion damages fund. Finally, on Day 87, the leak was plugged.

Every twist and turn of this national crisis played out on television, radio, print media and social media. And three-and-one-half years later, BP's corporate reputation still is mired in the fallout of the oil spill. Even after the flurry of media interest has faded, the damage from many crises takes years to repair.

Thankfully, most reputational crises aren't this dramatic.

Politics and sports are rich with examples of tarnished images: Lance Armstrong, Arnold Schwarzenegger, Anthony Weiner, Miley Cyrus, Tiger Woods, Charlie Sheen, John Edwards, Marion Jones, among others. Thanks to blogs, Facebook and Twitter, these scandals are global fodder for the chatterati – and good cocktail conversation. Sadly, celebrity and politico infidelity, lewd behavior and drug abuse often receive more attention than crises that truly affect the quality of life, such as recent problems in the financial industry.

For example, Justin Bieber sparked controversy with an April 2013 Facebook post.

> "Truly inspiring to be able to come here. Anne was a great girl. Hopefully she would have been a belieber."
>
>> Justin Bieber's comment in guest book of the Anne Frank House, Amsterdam (posted on Facebook page of Anne Frank House April 13, 2013)

The posting generated more than 3,000 comments on the Anne Frank House Facebook page. Most were appalled at Bieber's hubris and lack of sensitivity, not to mention his failure to grasp the courage of this young woman. It sparked a firestorm on Twitter where Bieber has nearly 47 million followers. That is not a typo, there really so many beliebers that the 19-year-old Canadian pop star and YouTube creation believes that traditional media isn't important to his publicity.

> A tweet by @rickgervais summed the controversy up: "I agree with Justin Bieber. Anne Frank would've loved his stuff. It's perfect for being played really really quietly so no one can hear it." (April 14, 2013)

Many called for the celebrity to apologize or acknowledge his lack of sensitivity and understanding of history. Instead, on April 15, two days later, Bieber only felt compelled to post photos of himself shirtless on Twitter.

Impact? The "crisis" faded, just like most crises do. Bieber, perhaps because of his youth and that of his fan base, was forgiven for being insensitive. Many crises are not so simplistic and require thoughtful, sincere and sometimes frequent responses.

Story-Telling in a Crisis

Definition of a crisis: *Any situation that is threatening or could threaten to harm people or property, seriously interrupt business, damage reputation and/or negatively impact stock value or an individual's reputation.*

The Social Media 4EVR definition of a crisis: *a specific, unexpected and or unorthodox event or series of events that drive high levels of uncertainty and provide both opportunities and threats to the organization's culture and top-level goals.*

Crises typically come in one of two flavors: smoldering or disaster. A smoldering crisis is an issue or situation that may develop into a full crisis affecting reputation. These are crisis situations you can anticipate. Lance Armstrong's doping scandal and Anthony Weiner's photo forays on Twitter are good examples. These individuals knew they were engaging in risky behavior but did harm anyway.

Sudden vs. Smoldering Crises

Both individuals and corporations can plan for the worst-case scenario (fraud, product failures, etc.) and take steps to prepare for and then mitigate a crisis when it happens. In fact, two-thirds of crises over the past decade have been smoldering, according to the Institute for Crisis Management, and therefore should have been anticipated and possibly prevented.

These issues are sometimes termed "Iceberg" because the bulk of the problem begins out of sight and "under the water." But with thoughtful assessment, smoldering crises can be identified in advance and managed before they become full crisis situations in the public domain. No matter which metaphor you choose, these types of crises typically start small, can be avoided, and are difficult to recover from if the crisis does manifest itself.

The second type of crisis is "sudden" and commonly called a disaster. A sudden crisis can be natural or man-made, ranging from a subway bombing or building fire to an earthquake or hurricane. Like a smoldering crisis, you should identify and plan for sudden crisis in advance.

Regardless of the type of crisis, there are three primary characters: the victim, the villain and the vindicator. In other words, who has been harmed or is perceived to have been harmed (victim), who (allegedly) caused the harm (villain) and who can remedy the harm (vindicator). The vindicator is the person acting on behalf of the victim to achieve some form of justice. These characters are integral to the crisis story.

These characters can be used to illustrate the challenge of reputation management. For years, 7-time Tour de France cycling champion Lance Armstrong portrayed himself as the victim of vicious attacks on his credibility by villains (his competitors, and the international cycling union, among others), and his teammates and supporters played the role of vindicators by validating Armstrong's story. He successfully fought doping allegations by telling a consistent story.

At least 24 times, Armstrong passed unannounced drug tests. But finally, in the fall of 2012, enough evidence was amassed to prove that he was actually the villain – a liar and a cheat who perpetrated a complex doping scheme. He sought Oprah Winfrey as his vindicator when he finally admitted publicly to his illegal behavior, but it was too late. His act of contrition came after he had suffered great loss of reputation, his winnings, and several endorsements.

Twitter erupted with drug jokes and skepticism, but not sympathy. Armstrong was stripped of his Tour de France titles. Corporate sponsors like Nike severed their ties with Armstrong. He was forced to step down at LIVESTRONG, the cancer foundation he created. Today, Armstrong continues to argue his case in court.

There are any number of "characters" involved in crisis situations. A frame of reference that could help puts them in three categories: villain, victim and vindicator, or the "Three Vs."

For more on these characters, Table 6 examines the response behaviors of each type of character.

CRISIS: A FRAME OF REFERENCE

Table 6

Victim	Who has been harmed (or perceived to be harmed)	The Three Vs are characters in a crisis who appear or are implied. Even if their roles are not explicitly defined, the audience knows who these characters are through the way the story is told.
Villain	Who (allegedly) caused the harm	
Vindicator	Who is acting on behalf of the victim to correct the harm that was done or achieve some form of justice	

News No Longer Breaks, it Tweets

While Armstrong illustrates a catastrophic outcome to reputation, you can successfully mitigate the damage or other negative effects by being empathetic, truthful, and available for comment.

An organization's or individual's reputation is often its most valuable asset. As a result, when that reputation comes under attack, protecting and defending it becomes the highest priority for all stakeholders. This is particularly true in today's 24/7 news cycle, which is driven by government investigations, Congressional hearings, litigation, and "gotcha" journalism. Moreover, the 24/7 news cycle is also fueled by unregulated/unrestricted commentary, online media, blogs, and other non-traditional outlets. Due to this vast audience, if the media firestorm is not properly monitored and managed it can overwhelm your ability to respond effectively to the demands of a crisis. Social media has a multiplier effect on the crisis. It can accelerate the markets, stakeholders, and challenges that each company or organization has to address.

The best illustration is the one that catapulted Twitter to its status as a *breaking* news channel – the Twitpic from the US Airways plane that crashed in the Hudson River on January 15, 2009.[1] A ferry commuter's tweet demonstrated the significance of social media, Twitter in particular, to break news and set the storyline for traditional media.

Today, it is common to have a top tweets or Twitter feed scrolling during a newscast. In fact, the two media have become dependent upon each other to report news and reactions.

"http://twitpic.com/135xa - There's a plane in the Hudson. I'm on the ferry going to pick up the people. Crazy." jkrums on Twitpic

After more than 7,000 views, Twitpic crashed. Subsequently, Janis Krums became a Twitter sensation and his photo became the first image shown on TV. Twitter catapulted the platform to become a leading source for breaking news and crisis response. As *Silicon Alley Insider* reported, "Thirty-four minutes after Krums posted his photo, MSNBC interviewed him live on TV as a witness."[2]

"News no longer breaks, it tweets," says Andrea Obston, crisis communications expert.

For more on responding to a crisis, see Hillary JM Topper's article at the end of this chapter. After reading that entry, you'll also find tips for crisis communication success from Jeff Lanza.

Managing a Crisis

"People expect companies to respond to crises at the same speed they learn about them, a speed defined by social media, smart phones and an infinite number of 'reporters,'" says Bob Winslow, FleishmanHillard's managing director of practice groups.[3] "Whether addressing data breaches, cyber-attacks, product recalls or activists' campaigns, companies that have time-tested strategic counsel and access to the best communications tools will better navigate any crisis affecting public safety and their reputation."

Simply put: in a crisis, you must respond quickly and effectively using both traditional and social media channels. If you aren't first to tell the story, the reporters and social chatter will define the story for you.

"Tell it all. Tell it fast. Tell it yourself," says Dawn Doty, vice president and partner at LPR, former PR adviser to the Tiger Woods Foundation.[4]

The first step in preparing for or responding to a crisis is conducting an inventory of your vulnerabilities and then preparing response scenarios for each. This allows you to identify and clean up problems or issues before they explode onto the front page of the paper, lead the evening news, or trend on Twitter.

The next step then should be obvious – make a crisis plan. Be it a smoldering crisis or sudden disaster, you can anticipate scenarios that may impact your or your company negatively. Plan your work so that when the time comes, you can work your plan.

Third, as part of your plan define the channels and the tactics your response will use. These include traditional media and most commonly Twitter and Facebook. However, there may be instances where YouTube or Instagram are essential to tell your story. If you or your corporation has a Twitter presence, identify the hashtag (#topic) that will help you monitor the conversation.

© Can Stock Photo Inc./fotoscool

Finally, measure what you have accomplished.

In today's social media environment, your communications should be two-way. Pushing your messages via news releases, tweets and Facebook postings often are not enough. Determine how you will respond to criticism, answer customer questions and engage with key audiences.

Gartner, a technology research and consulting firm, issued a report in 2012 finding that 75 percent of organizations will integrate social media into their crisis plans by 2015.[5] "Enterprises simply cannot afford to ignore social media as a crisis communications tool," said Andrew Walls, research vice president at Gartner. "In many cases, social media may represent the only available means of locating and contacting personnel; providing stakeholders with the information and assistance they need; informing citizens, customers and partners of product/service availability; and taking other business-critical actions following a disruptive event."

Stakeholders often remember more about how you handle a crisis situation than the actual crisis itself.

For proof of that statement, look no further than the legendary Tylenol case or the infamous Exxon Valdez fiasco. Both of these happened more than 15 years ago, but every PR student is still taught about these cases. Particularly, students are taught how the reputations of each company still bear the impact, either good or bad, because of how the crises were handled.

The key to effectively handle a crisis is the quality and integrity of your crisis plan and your expertise at implementing it.

Today, you must factor in social media when preparing a crisis plan. A crisis can start in one of these channels – criticism in a blog or chat group, a tweeted picture of private anatomy, a faux Twitter account. An offline crisis can also be remediated by using social media.

A 2013 study by the University of Missouri School of Journalism finds that Facebook is an effective tool to solve or lessen the severity of a crisis.[6] The channel is more about storytelling than the facts, which the Bieber example mentioned previously demonstrates. The "crisis" may have reinforced perceptions about unworldly or unknowledgeable teens, but it did little to negatively impact his image.

However, most crises of image or reputation do require a response. Lance Armstrong is a great illustration of that requirement.

Building trust

Your brand and credibility are at stake, so you need the public's trust. In preparing, one of the first issues to consider is the level of disclosure given, or the scope and nature of the problem. There are many points of view regarding this matter. From acknowledging the issue to providing full details, each company or individual goes about this in a different way. However, most crisis communications veterans will tell you that for the most part, the story and many of the gory details will come out eventually!

Football legend Bear Bryant once said, "In a crisis, don't hide behind anything or anybody. They are going to find you anyway."

#Cruisefromhell

Most famously known as the "poop cruise," for five days in February 2013, 4,200 passengers were stranded on Carnival Cruise Lines Triumph in the Gulf of Mexico. Due to a fire in the engine room, the Triumph was adrift at sea with significant dining and sanitation problems. Passengers took to

Twitter, Facebook and Instagram to document long lines for food and graphic images of sewage backups and overflowing buckets of poop. CNN broadcast coverage of the crisis. And the #cruisefromhell hashtag trended on Twitter.

In response, Carnival updated its Facebook page 20 times and sent more than 60 tweets during the crisis. Its efforts at information sharing and transparency should be commended. But this was a traditional crisis response, relying on one-way communications, when today's social media landscape requires customer engagement.

Carnival's social media messaging focused on sharing links to news releases or posting factual updates, which did include $500 and a flight home once the Triumph arrived in Mobile, Alabama. But pushing information via social media, such as tweeting from officials @CarnivalCruise about complimentary bathrobes, failed to engage customer complaints directly via these important channels.

More egregious, however, was the nearly three days before the CEO Gerry Cahill made a public, press statement about the fire or Carnival's rescue plans.[7] "The single most important factor in mitigating the depth and breadth of a crisis, and preserving the organization's reputation over the long term, is the attitude of the person at the top," says Joan Gladstone, APR, Fellow PRSA, in *The Public Relations Strategist*.

When crisis strikes, an organization's response should be immediate and should be delivered from executive leadership. While Carnival began responding promptly via social media, its key spokesperson – the chief executive – was absent. This was a significant misstep and a missed opportunity to demonstrate that the crisis was being addressed from the highest levels of the organization.

Cahill, when he did speak, took responsibility for the crisis and addressed steps to remediate the situation. But he should have been heard from within an hour of the crisis, even if only to confirm the incident, note that safety protocols are being observed and that the company will work to resolve the situation. Instead, it was approximately 60 hours before Cahill spoke with media.

Here's a summary of the key steps in handling a crisis:

1. Gather and verify the facts from all reliable sources to assess the risk and liability to your reputation, the organization and/or its executives.

2. Create a unique plan, or adapt your existing crisis plan if possible, for the situation and the specific players involved.

3. Define the social media channels that will be most helpful in a crisis.

4. Measure the effectiveness of your plan.

As previously noted, the major impact of the Internet is the speed at which things move and the global reach stories can have. Things are not as they were in previous days when media deadlines and publishing schedules gave you more time to think things over and respond.

Mark Twain once wrote, "A lie is halfway around the world before the truth has its pants on."

This quote has added significance in the current, internet-driven media environment. Social media's multiplier effect has changed the time to react from hours to minutes. But one of the challenges you may find is that many corporate executives, athletes, celebrities and their advisors (e.g. lawyers) may not have adjusted to the new pace. This may slow you, and your response time, down which can be a serious mistake in the modern environment of crisis management.

Crises Move Fast

Crises move faster than ever. Rumors, mis-statements, and false allegations move at breakneck speed. In some cases, these achieve credibility because you are not aware of them or have not properly addressed them.

This examination of crisis communication shows how important advanced preparation can be. The primary requirement is to have a plan in place that can get you through the first few hours or days of a crisis. Then, deliberate and timely response is critical. Creating interaction also gives real time feedback about the crisis communication plan so adjustments can be made if necessary.

Crisis Communication Endnotes

1: http://news.cnet.com/8301-1023_3-10143736-93.html

2: http://www.businessinsider.com/2009/1/us-airways-crash-rescue-picture-citizen-jouralism-twitter-at-work

3: http://www.prnewswire.com/news-releases/fleishmanhillard-certifies-crisis-counselors-in-innovative-methodology-214784381.html

4: http://www.linhartpr.com/blog/crisis-communications-and-the-golden-hour-the-difference-between-tiger-woods-and-captain-sullenberger/

5: http://www.gartner.com/newsroom/id/1935519

6: http://munews.missouri.edu/news-releases/2013/0903-facebook-use-by-organizations-during-crises-helps-public-image-mu-study-finds/

7: http://carnival-news.com/2013/02/12/carnival-cruise-lines-president-and-ceo-gerry-cahills-press-conference-comment-regarding-carnival-triumph/

∞

Responding to negative feedback on social networking
By Hillary JM Topper, MPA

Many clients still don't want to jump into social networking sites because of the fear of negative feedback.

So here's what I tell them.

Imagine that you walk into your favorite shoe store. You try on a beautiful pair of shoes and buy them. You take them home and discover that the heel is damaged. You go back to the store the next day feeling frustrated and the owner tells you that he's sorry; he can't take the shoes back. You leave the store angry, but the storeowner has no idea how mad you are. You proceed to call all of your friends who go to that store and tell them to never go back. As the weeks go by, the storeowner sees less and less business. He doesn't understand why. Eventually, he closes down.

Now, take that same scenario and imagine that the person wrote something on the store's Facebook wall. At least the storeowner knows where the damage is coming from. One can have controls in place and alleviate the negativity by turning it into positivity.

A positive spin

About a year ago, I went to the Tanger Outlets in Deer Park, Long Island during the weekend of Fourth of July with my parents. We decided to go after seeing a coupon for a discount book in the local newspaper. After picking up our coupon books, I tried to use the coupons at several stores. However, at each store I went to, the employees told us that the coupons were not valid because it was a holiday weekend and that we couldn't use coupons on items that were already discounted.

I was mad. I felt like it was a bait and switch! I wrote a blog entry and posted it for all of my friends to see. I tweeted it out and posted it on Facebook. And, after I did that, I felt better. A few weeks later, I received a letter from Tanger's corporate office in North Carolina. They wrote me to apologize for my inconvenience and offered me a $25 gift card. After that gesture, I rescinded my blog post, and I told everyone what happened. So Tanger Outlets received positive press from me just by responding.

What should you do if someone provides negative feedback about you or your company?

- Acknowledge it immediately. Don't delete or ignore negative statements unless they are cruel. There are some people who write malicious statements that aren't constructive or make accusations that aren't accurate. If someone says something, then respond to him or her.
- Don't get defensive. By becoming defensive, you will just escalate the attack. Try to talk in a direct way and be transparent.
- Take it off-line. Move the conversation off-line if you can. Then, talk to the person via email, direct message or telephone. Perhaps you can come to an agreement that will suit both parties, such as a gift certificate or a refund.
- Be honest and sincere. Explain why you can or can't take a certain action but remember that social media is about customer service as much as it is about being social.
- Follow up. After you resolve an issue, make sure to follow up and let the other person know that you care about them and want to make sure they are satisfied.
- Don't remove the post. Unless it is something mean that doesn't have anything to do with your product or service, don't delete the negative comments. If it's a direct attack against you personally and isn't constructive, then it's OK to take it down.

Reprinted with permission from *Public Relations Tactics* (Aug. 2, 2013)

About the Author

Hilary JM Topper, MPA is the president and CEO of HJMT Public Relations in Melville, N.Y., and in Rochester. Her firm focuses on getting people to know your business. In addition, she is a blogger at HilaryTopper.com, ARunnersDiary.com, GoogleGlassPix.com and HJMT.com. She is also a Google Glass Explorer and the host of an online radio show found at blogtalkradio.com/hilarytopper. You can reach out to her on Twitter @Hilary25.

∞

Crisis Communication: 12 Tips for Success

Provided by Jeff Lanza, jefflanza@thelanzagroup.com
Reprinted with permission

1. Communicate with employees before delivering messages to other stakeholders.
   a. Remember that employees are an important stakeholder in your communications and should share in the challenge and vision for the future.
   b. Stay well connected to your employees – everyone is responsible for shepherding your organization back to normalcy during a crisis.
2. Don't underestimate the power of the media to control the agenda.
   a. Be ready to tell your side of the story – fast.
   b. Complacency and inertia can lead to communication failure.
3. Build relationships with your local HR writers and bloggers.
   a. It becomes less likely that stories will be published without your input.
   b. Have a documented media contact procedure in your organization. Employees responsible for media responses need to be available 24/7.
4. Be the first and most credible source of information.
   a. Deliver information before people get it through less than credible sources.
   b. If you have bad news, deliver it first - it is always more palatable if it comes from the source.
5. Be ready and able to deliver information through multiple portals.
   a. Unleash the power of instant communication through the use of texting, Twitter and Facebook.
   b. Update your corporate Web site as quickly as possible in a crisis.
6. Monitor what is being "reported" about your company on social sites.
   a. Respond in an appropriate and non-defensive manner.
   b. Correct inaccuracies and embellishments.

7. Don't just say "we can't comment."
   a. If you can't discuss an issue explain the reason.
   b. You can always talk about "the process," if you don't have the facts yet.
8. Don't cover-up, mislead or deceive any of your stakeholders.
   a. Be truthful – a cover-up will create problems that outlive the actual crisis.
   b. The media have ways to get to the truth – it is always better if it comes from you directly.
9. Be message driven in your communications.
   a. A message is a point, theme or idea.
   b. Messages should be clear and concise, relevant and include action steps if necessary.
10. Be empathetic to those affected by the crisis.
    a. Talk from the heart.
    b. People remember how you made them feel, not exactly what you said.
11. Look for exaggerations and embellishments.
    a. Set the record straight.
    b. If you don't correct the information as stated, you implicitly accept that is true.
12. Use success stories and accomplishments to boost morale and to set sights on the future.
    a. Remind employees of the positive things your organization has accomplished.
    b. A continued focus on the positive will help diminish the negative effects the crisis has created.

Chapter 11: SM4EVR - Accept the Challenge!

∞

Social Media 4EVR

This chapter is, in the truest social networking sense, a call to action. There are any number of reasons not to participate, and there are any number of reasons that participation should be beneficial. Similarly, it is almost certain that whatever social networking life people are leading now will not cause catastrophe if left in its present state. But there's more to social networking than that. There is the vibrant, ongoing, dynamic digital conversation that is all at once enriching, educating, exciting, and surprising. Yes, that digital conversation will be fine without you, but we would not have written this book if we didn't think this was something you should be involved in. If you are participating now, your participation can get better and be more effective. If you're not participating, you can get involved. If your hesitation is about privacy and security, there are controls to help you. The Social Media 4EVR approach offers the same effective tools and techniques regardless of the platform you choose: Facebook, LinkedIn, Twitter, Pinterest, Myspace, Google+, YouTube, Instagram, Tumblr, Blogger, WordPress, etc. It's about improving your social networking participation in ways that matter to the most important person: YOU!

∞

This book examines the "act" of social networking as a process and practice that will help you come together with people and communities to communicate and interact. The intent is to provide evidence of useful processes – a personal brand, analysis of options, and a social media plan – that work regardless of the common websites and specialized areas one might employ to share, access, download, provide and discuss a variety of types of information. This should start you on a journey to find tools and tactics that can affect creativity, idea exchange and communication effectiveness.

We introduced you to policy in Chapter 8, demonstrating that you need principles, rules and guidelines that allow you to reach long-term goals. This is a part of the organization's culture that influences major decisions and actions.

Effective policies are required before we can be effective with the next important social networking considerations: trust and risk.

Focus on Trust

In terms of trust, if you perceive that there is a benefit, you will be more inclined to participate and collaborate with others. Trust and perception are the same for others you may encounter. Participation then boils down to whether there is a real or perceived benefit in terms of return on the investment of the time or attention spent participating. The benefit could also be the availability of new challenges or new connections.

Risk is a little tougher, and it is affected by barriers to social networking covered in Chapter 6. Social networking can introduce risks, especially to companies. Organizational risks can include compliance with regulatory requirements, reputational damage, information leakage, loss of intellectual property, malware attacks, copyright infringement, and privacy that may be harmful to operations and/or corporate image.

Personal risks have some of the same characteristics, like the danger of damaging reputation (personal brand) or problems with posting information that exposes more of one's personal life than intended (information leakage). Hackers can cause problems for individuals, as can postings by others that are inaccurate or inflammatory.

There are actions you can take to manage these risks, starting with owning the truth about your reputation and activities on a site or platform where you have control. Experts recommend using strong privacy and security settings and avoiding suspicious third-party applications. When networking, treat everything you post as public.

Most important, carefully assess the people you share with, and then assess them again. In your social networking activities, you might use a "friend of a friend" system for vetting people. If they know or are connected to someone in your network whom you trust and respect, then maybe you can accept connecting with them. Without that, it might not be wise to accept someone you haven't met.

Take Some Risks

Having said all of that, you might want to take some risks. There are just too many people involved in the social networking adventure who are too compelling to ignore or delete or refuse or turn away from. Once the adventure has captured your full attention, push forward with privacy controls at the ready and take on the FULL social networking challenge!

You might want to risk the time that people complain is excessive because you can imagine the benefits. The communication advantage gained saves more time than you spend, so it may be worth it.

Another key objection deals with losing control of the message. Two points here:

(1) You may not want to control the message because at any given time you won't have all the answers; and

(2) No one ever controls the message for more than a few, fleeting moments.

Keep in mind that the digital conversation keeps moving and you have to stay with it. If you wait until you need to know, this uncontrollable medium may be moving too fast for you to engage at the time you need to engage. For instance, you may be trying to address another group of popular complaints:

- Negative comments;
- Incorrect information; or
- Unnecessary information.

Our answer to these complaints and to wading through digital conversations is the same: you may have to filter through a lot of junk to find a jewel of information. But when you find that jewel, isn't it all worth the time and effort? How many great inventions failed first, and how many times did they fail? There are similarities here.

Of course, some believe in the old saying: "To each his own." However, we continue to be excited about the boundless opportunities to discover social networking in all its glory. That's what Social Media 4EVR offers. It offers thought processes and planning practices that address goals, establish roles, and seek feedback and verification that the social networking approach is working.

This is an opportunity to use one or all of the 4 pillars of social media to create and nurture an exciting, energetic approach to your participation. Social Media 4EVR also offers significant change in social media literature focused on helping individuals, businesses, government, elected officials, and educators. This approach allows the destination, not the path or platform, to be the focus of social networking participation.

© Can Stock Photo Inc./thesupe87

Organizations and individuals should look beyond near-term personal or financial benefits and leverage short-term costs (either time or expenses) that promote positive social and environmental change. As social capital theory teaches, there are ways that the efficiency of society can be improved by facilitating coordinated actions.

Social Media 4EVR can help government organizations and elected officials at different levels, for instance, who use social media to actively listen to citizens and who use that information to constantly monitor existing services and develop new initiatives. Educators can benefit from a better understanding of social media platforms to help students improve their online interactions using the goal-setting focus and social media plan advocated in these pages. Students could open up a whole new world of interactions by moving their frame of reference from solely which platform to use – Facebook, LinkedIn, Twitter, etc. – to a view of goal achievement and audience targeting.

Seeking Value

Social Media 4EVR presents planning practices, talks about measurement and feedback, and actively seeks value and accomplishment in social networking. The value we see is for private citizens and for organizations. Citizens can share constructive ideas and opinions and enjoy active roles in their activities, while organizations can listen, monitor and engage in digital conversations to enhance activities. These benefits are important to taking advantage of services, developing plans of action and creating and maintaining quality relationships.

By stressing the importance of building capital and accepting the value propositions that drive social networking, we've provided you a plan and a way ahead for meaningful participation. By now, you should be able to identify your social networking expectations so that you can create value through a reasonable investment of time and effort. The tools and techniques provided will serve you well, and you should get better and better at using a plan to leverage your personal or professional brand.

This journey demonstrates how the destination of the social networking endeavor, not the path or platform, can be the driving focus of participation. The baseline of a networking system allows participation on several social media platforms with a consistent persona and voice across all.

Taking advantage of one or more of the 4 pillars of social media strategy – communication, collaboration, education and entertainment – is another key theme. Using the Social Media 4EVR approach can lead to valuable engagements that build on content, define your brand, create social capital, and establish your reputation.

The process started with a sound strategy contained in a great plan that ensures the most effective communication, interaction and need satisfaction via social media. It continued with audience analysis and selection, focusing on audience information gathering: where do they get their information and with whom do they exchange information. It's always important to find out where the target audience is posting, texting, viewing video, or sharing images.

An approach of action, response and behavior as a two-way exchange is what social networking requires. In this way, real value transcends time and space and leads to a continuity of connection that is priceless. These are all important considerations for you before moving to a planning phase that sets a road map for your efforts.

Planning and Engagements

Personal and business planning are keys to success in social media efforts. Planning facilitates open, unfettered communication to discuss ideas, publish news, ask questions and share links. It also helps people expand their audience, finding people who are like-minded to enhance reputation.

If you have a plan before you engage in social networking, it can help protect you from dangers, threats or hesitations that are everywhere in "social media land." Also, a good plan can serve as a corrective tool to make adjustments to make networking activities even more rewarding.

Now you have an online conversation that is structured in unconventional ways; it is organic and complex. It connects people and businesses, allowing engagements and shared content. This signals a valuable return on the investment of time. As stated earlier, even if there is simply a perception of benefit, users may be more inclined to participate, or they may be moved to increase their participation levels. This value-based examination is what powers our approach to social networking and individual planning.

Social Media 4EVR examines social networking in a variety of ways. It analyzes adjustments to engagement thought processes utilizing a non-traditional approach. We don't focus on getting started and learning the "how;" we seek out the "why." Why are you getting involved, what do you intend to accomplish, and what will be your measuring stick for when you've achieved your goals?

This book provides some history that is relevant to social networking. Social media has changed the way we read and disseminate information, using many-to-many models to energize and speed up communications at all levels. Even one-on-one conversations can take on a new energy through social media. This medium focuses on humanizing and personalizing stories specifically for the people we want to reach, allowing us to share information and build strong relationships.

We've offered a little history to get you started. The history focuses on adoption of innovation, which addresses decision processes that occur at the individual level. It also focuses on how users are attracted to a system and how their behavior is affected. Literature on innovation adoption (2007), the technology acceptance model (Davis 1986, Kwon and Wen 2010), governing by network (Goldsmith and Eggers 2004), social capital theory (Putnam 1993), social network analysis (Hatala 2006), and trust were explored to provide a good foundation. The history is offered because, as they say, "How can you know where you're going if you don't know where you've been?

Social media theory is a part of the learning here, because digital conversations are active whether one is listening or not. The theoretical background provides reference for the thought processes necessary to be successful in social networking. After all, networking is about, on some level, enhancing positive perceptions and addressing negative perceptions. This book focuses on these theories: innovation adoption, governing by network, building trust, social capital, social learning, social network analysis, and the Hawthorne effect.

Engagements help to bring social networking to life, interacting with people to share valuable information and resources. They offer enhanced performance and allow your digital "self" to be seen and heard across platforms. Then you can coordinate all efforts, manage the tension that can come with collaboration, and overcome many of the limitations of social networking abilities and knowledge that one might face.

Employ your intended end state or mission to guide you in the process you select, and let that process guide your efforts. The process should help you ask the right questions about the outcome you seek. Then select your network partners wisely to ensure you can build long-standing, mutually beneficial relationships. The focus of these interactions is shared value that creates ties that endure because of dependable communication channels, coordinated activities between network participants, and the establishment of trusting relationships.

Beyond just the technology, social networking success also requires vigilance in addressing interactivity with the people you value, examining and improving your processes constantly, and aligning values and trust to complement each other. These concerns and responsibilities, when managed effectively, can open the door to the enormous value available to participants.

Engage and deliver great content that advances your social networking initiatives. This generates interest and delivers social capital to your audience. Listen and understand what the community says in the feedback you receive. Social capital requires establishing purposeful relationships to generate and receive tangible social, psychological, emotional and economic benefits in short or long terms.

Set yourself up for social media success by staying familiar with and using the 4 pillars – communication, collaboration, education and entertainment. The pillars are helpful for any end state and are relevant whether you're building a trusted environment, connecting with a new person or group for short- or long-term purposes, or working to become a thought leader in your industry or community. Pick your pillar or pillars wisely and be consistent with your efforts.

Help yourself with interactive listening. The requirements for interactive listening, as listed in a social media benchmarking study (Brown, Alkadry et al. 2013):

- Look beyond connecting with people and focus on building meaningful relationships with key stakeholders;
- Develop a strong capability to listen to and understand all audiences;
- Trust and empower employees and strive for increased transparency in activities;
- Coordinate the organization's messages and goals into a unified voice across all channels; and
- Be flexible to adapt to and respond to stakeholders in real time.

A Revolution

The social media revolution, if you want to call it that, continues at a dizzying pace. New discoveries every day require that we listen to the digital conversation at every opportunity. Being strategic and staying in touch with the digital conversation helps us engage stakeholders and friends using the channels they prefer.

Personal and professional connections are based on levels of trust. For example, organizations may provide "social media time" as part of processes to create new business, enhance innovation, and improve the work and personal lives of employees. Those processes require that organizations seek interactions that are administratively effective and professionally accountable. Therefore, social networking is a two-step, voluntary process where people accept or reject participation, and then determine levels of activity that suit their needs and/or lifestyles.

Whatever pillar you choose, be sure to create enabling conditions that allow success in networking activities through four keys:

- Facilitate dialogue with an organized and capable community that is engaged in ongoing digital conversations that create shared value and build social capital;
- Identify communication champions to keep conversations alive through people who are not only engaged in the conversation but who energize it and even take it to other communities to inject other points of view;
- Ensure contextual and cultural information appropriateness to foster conversations that are relevant and appropriate for the community of interest based on demographic values of the community and cultural considerations; and
- Access to information is crucial to helping the other keys work, so your community understands your approach and so that your actions are transparent and timely.

Make the revolution work for you through branding. Branding can make compelling testimonials about who you are and can provide important details about your expertise. Pay attention to the differences in personal brand and corporate brand, so you don't violate any employer-related rules. Branding is key to community building where one introduces, nurtures and solidifies social networking "marketable" skills and capabilities.

Again, just be sure to keep the lines between corporate and personal separate. Ensure that there is clear delineation of comment and identity between what is personal, what is professional, what is public and what is private.

In the end, be sure to "stay in your lane" and be careful with the information you exchange. If you are the information "owner," by all means share. But if the information is out of your expertise or not part of your job, it is better to let someone else provide it to the public.

Understanding the importance of trust is key to building and delivering your brand to your community of interest. Intra-organizational trust is the trust people in an organization have in one another that creates and nurtures social bonds and collaboration in social networking activities. It is vital to achieving collective receptivity to and exploitation of interactions in social media.

Trust is also necessary for developing relationship dependence, satisfaction and commitment. These trusting relationships lead people to give most people the benefit of the doubt, and can be extended to people one does not know from direct experience.

Once you've created that personal brand, analyze it. Assess the effectiveness of the brand by asking tough questions. Are you answering questions on social media sites, and do you share links, videos or other content with your audiences? Do you post slide decks to sites like Slideshare? Do you upload advice or how-to videos, or do you write valuable content in a blog and answer resulting comments? Finally, do you invite, connect, link, etc., with people who share your interests?

Finally, employ the three Cs of personal branding: Clear, Consistent and Collaborative. Always be clear about who you are and who you are not and don't compromise that position for any reason. Be consistent in expressing your brand across all communication vehicles you employ. Take a collaborative approach to create regular, valuable content, because strong brands are always visible to their target audiences.

Social Media Evolution

The social media evolution (Table 3 in Chapter 6) that moves from visitor to elder is a way to determine what your participation is, what you want it to be, and what it could be. Decide who you want to be: we showed the social media evolution that moves through visitors, lurkers, novices, insiders, leaders and elders. Once you decide who you are, you should take a formal approach to your participation which consists of four actions; joining, listening, speaking and interacting.

Join a community or engage with your stakeholders, using the basics of your personal profile to introduce yourself. Take time to listen to what they are saying and understand what the community of interest is all about. Once you have a handle on what's going on, speak by letting the audience or community of interest know more about you. At this stage, you can start to interact by sharing information and ideas and getting to know more about your new-found friends.

Every day, we read about the problems of fraudulent interactions, spam and virus attacks, and identity theft. Negative comments about our public persona or about the information we post present a threat that many want to avoid at all costs. But don't let those negatives keep you from the benefits that social media offers.

Yes, there are perils out there, but there are safeguards available. For instance, identifying your audience, keeping a watch on privacy controls, managing your personal brand, and properly reviewing your posts for relevance, accuracy and propriety are ways to stay "safe."

Policy

When you set out to develop – or interpret and follow – an institutional social media policy, two considerations are paramount. First, don't be a puppet master. An organization cannot control individual conservations, but you can set values and expectations. Second, involve all corporate functions in the development of the policy. Our hope is that the public relations executives and team are leading the process and that members from all other departments will play an important role in forming, teaching and implementing the policy. When forming the policy team, you will want to select a cross section of individuals from throughout the organization – senior management and mid-level and junior staff. This will help ensure that the policy is informed by different experiences and engagement with social media.

Leverage the policy available to inform a strategic approach to social media planning. Your plan can deliver quality results through research and clearly defined goals and audiences.

A social media plan should contain several parts, which includes an introduction, a statement of goals, a list of objectives and an identification of the intended audience. Include a clear statement of the communication strategy, the intended channels for communicating, and the tone of voice of the communication that you will set. Remember, tone and voice are about delivering all your messages and ensuring they sound like they are coming from the same person each time. Next add tactics and timing and consider key success factors. Key success factors are direct access to your community of interest, an ability to show value in what you provide, an ability to discuss the benefits of continued interaction, and an opportunity to use a "push" approach to create a "pull" approach. In other words, start by reaching to them, and then show the value of them reaching to you. Finish with measurement of your efforts.

Crisis Communication

Crises can be smoldering, long brewing, or they can come at you suddenly. No matter what kind of crisis you face, remember that you can plan in advance so that you can ensure you respond quickly, truthfully and frequently. So, in all situations you need to be fast, honest and responsive.

The other key consideration in crisis communication deals with who is involved. Chapter 10 talks about a crisis in terms of the victim, the villain and the vindicator and defines those roles. The Three Vs are characters in a crisis who appear or are implied. Even if their roles are not explicitly defined, the audience knows who these characters are through the way the story is told.

What Does It All Mean?

So, that sums up our social networking journey.

Now, we should all be focused on trust that grows from one participant committing to an action with one or more other participants based on a belief that the action will lead to a good outcome. We take the risk based on a belief that others will act in an admirable and ethical way as they listen and respond to our information sharing activities. We're building an understanding of social capital to show how parties can benefit personally and professionally, and how we can work together to address problems and solve them collectively.

Focusing on the end state of your participation paves the way to arrive at a destination of your choosing. In turn, it leads to managing expectations to share value and get a worthy return on the time and effort you commit to social networking.

As you continue your social networking activities, we wish you good luck and hope you will keep an eye on Social Media 4EVR. We will keep discovering great things about social networking, and we hope you will follow us on the exciting road to social networking success through unfettered communication.

Good luck!

Bibliography

Ajzen, I. and M. Fishbein (1980). Understanding Attitudes and Predicting Human Behavior. Englewood, Prentice Hall.

Akdere, M. and P. B. Roberts (2008). "Economics of Social Capital: Implications for Organizational Performance." Advances in Developing Human Resources 10(6): 802.

Bachmann, R., D. Knights and J. Sydow (2001). "Special Issue: Trust and control in organizational relations." Organization Studies 22(2).

Bandura, A. (1977). Social learning theory. Englewood Cliffs, N.J., Prentice Hall.

Bandura, A. (1986). Social foundations of thought and action: a social cognitive theory. Englewood Cliffs, N.J., Prentice-Hall.

Bearman, T. C., P. Guynup and S. N. Milevski (1985). "Information and Productivity." Journal of the American Society for Information Science (pre-1986) 36(6): 369.

Bolino, M. C., W. H. Turnley and J. M. Bloodgood (2002). "Citizenship Behavior and the Creation of Social Capital in Organizations." The Academy of Management Review 27(4): 505-522.

Borgatti, S. (2000). "Granovetter's theory of the strength of weak ties." Retrieved 23 May, 2009, from http://www.analytictech.com/networks/weakties.htm.

Brown, M., Sr. (2011). Social networking and individual performance: Examining predictors of participation Ph.D., Old Dominion University.

Brown, M., Sr., M. Alkadry and S. Resnick-Luetke (2013). "Social Networking and Individual Perceptions: Examining Predictors of Participation." Public Organization Review: 1-20.

Cerulo, K. A. (1990). "To Err Is Social: Network Prominence and Its Effects on Self-Estimation." Sociological Forum 5(4): 619-634.

Chung, K. S. K., L. Hossain and J. Davis (2007). Individual performance in knowledge intensive work through social networks. Proceedings of the 2007 ACM SIGMIS CPR conference on Computer personnel research: The global information technology workforce, St. Louis, Missouri, USA, ACM.

Cooper, R. K. (1997). "Applying Emotional Intelligence in the Workplace." Training & Development 51(12): 31-38.

Damanpour, F. and W. M. Evan (1984). "Organizational Innovation and Performance: The Problem of "Organizational Lag"." Administrative Science Quarterly 29(3): 392-409.

Damanpour, F. and S. Gopalakrishnan (1998). "Theories of organizational structure and innovation adoption: the role of environmental change." Journal of Engineering and Technology Management **15**(1): 1-24.

Damanpour, F., R. Walker and C. Avellaneda (2009). "Combinative Effects of Innovation Types and Organizational Performance: A Longitudinal Study of Service Organizations." The Journal of Management Studies **46**(4): 650.

Davis, F. D. (1986). A Technology Acceptance Model for Empirically Testing New End-User Information Systems: Theory and Results," doctoral dissertation. MIT Sloan School of Management, Cambridge, MA

Davis, F. D. (1989). "Perceived Usefulness, Perceived Ease of Use, and User Acceptance of Information Technology." MIS Quarterly **13**(3): 319-340.

Davis, T. R. V. and F. Luthans (1980). "A Social Learning Approach to Organizational Behavior." The Academy of Management Review **5**(2): 281-290.

Dennis, A. R. and J. S. Valacich (1994). "Group, Sub-Group, and Nominal Group Idea Generation: New Rules for a New Media?" Journal of Management **20**(4): 723-736.

Dirks, K. T. and D. L. Ferrin (2001). "The role of trust in organizational settings." Organization Science **12**(4): 450.

Eastin, M. S. and R. LaRose (2000). "Internet Self-Efficacy and the Psychology of the Digital Divide." Journal of Computer-Mediated Communication **6**(1): np.

Erickson, C. L. and S. M. Jacoby (2003). "The effects of employer networks on workplace innovation and training." Industrial & Labor Relations Review **56**(2): 203.

Ferrin, D. L. and K. T. Dirks (2003). "The use of rewards to increase and decrease trust: Mediating processes and differential effects." Organization Science **14**(1): 18.

Ferrin, D. L., K. T. Dirks and P. P. Shah (2006). "Direct and indirect effects of third-party relationships on interpersonal trust." Journal of Applied Psychology **91**(4): 870-883.

Field, J. (2003). Social Capital. London, Routledge.

Fishbein, M. and I. Ajzen (1975). Belief, Attitude, Intention, and Behavior: An Introduction to Theory and Research. Reading, MA, Addison-Wesley.

Fowler, S. W., T. B. Lawrence and E. A. Morse (2004). "Virtually Embedded Ties." Journal of Management **30**(5): 647-666.

Gambetta, D. (1988). Trust: making and breaking cooperative relations. New York, NY, USA, B. Blackwell.

Gladwell, M. (2002). The tipping point : how little things can make a big difference. Boston, Little, Brown.

Golbeck, J. A. (2005). Computing and applying trust in web-based social networks Ph.D., University of Maryland, College Park.

Goldsmith, S. and W. D. Eggers (2004). Governing by network: the new shape of the public sector. Washington, D.C., Brookings Institution Press.

Grey, C. and C. Garsten (2001). "Trust, Control and Post-Bureaucracy." Organization Studies 22(2): 229-250.

Hatala, J.-P. (2006). "Social Network Analysis in Human Resource Development: A New Methodology." Human Resource Development Review 5(1): 45.

Hatala, J.-P. and P. R. Fleming (2007). "Making Transfer Climate Visible: Utilizing Social Network Analysis to Facilitate the Transfer of Training." Human Resource Development Review 6(1): 33.

Hatala, J.-P. and J. G. Lutta (2009). "Managing Information Sharing Within an Organizational Setting: A Social Network Perspective." Performance Improvement Quarterly 21(4): 5.

Huy, Q. N. (1999). "Emotional Capability, Emotional Intelligence, and Radical Change." The Academy of Management Review 24(2): 325-345.

Igbaria, M. and M. Tan (1997). "The consequences of information technology acceptance on subsequent individual performance." Information & Management 32(3): 113-121.

Ivancevich, J. M., Konopaske, Robert, Matteson, Michael T. (2008). Organizational Behavior and Management. New York, McGraw-Hill/Irwin.

Kim, D. H. (1993). "The link between individual learning and organizational learning." Sloan Management Review 35(Fall): 379-500.

Kramer, R. M. (1996). Trust in organizations: Frontiers of theory and research. Thousand Oaks, Sage Publications.

Kulmann, T. M. (1988). "Adapting to Technical Change in the Workplace." Personnel 65(8): 67.

Kwon, O. and Y. Wen (2010). "An empirical study of the factors affecting social network service use." Computers in Human Behavior 26(2): 254-263.

Lane, C. and R. Bachmann (1998). Trust within and between organizations: Conceptual issues and empirical applications. New York, Oxford University Press.

Lasden, M. (1981). "Turning Reluctant Users on to Change." Computer Decisions 13(1): 92.

Leana, C. R. and H. J. v. Buren, III (1999). "Organizational Social Capital and Employment Practices." The Academy of Management Review 24(3): 538-555.

Luhmann, N. (1988). Familiarity, confidence, trust: Problems and alternatives. Trust: Making and breaking cooperative relations. D. Gambetta. New York, Basil Blackwell.

Lyytinen, K. and G. M. Rose (2003). "The Disruptive Nature of Information Technology Innovations: The Case of Internet Computing in Systems Development Organizations." MIS Quarterly **27**(4): 557-595.

Mahoney, M. J. and C. E. Thoresen (1974). Self-control: power to the person. Monterey, Calif., Brooks/Cole Pub. Co.

Makkonen, H. (2008). "Beyond Organizational Innovation Adoption: a Conceptual and Empirical Analysis " Journal of Business Market Management **2**(2): 63-77.

Marsh, W. (1990). "Meeting The Challenge Of Change." Australian Accountant **60**(1): 34.

Mayo, E. (1949). Hawthorne and the Western Electric Company: The Social Problems of an Industrial Civilisation. New York, Routledge.

McEvily, B., V. Perrone and A. Zaheer (2003). "Introduction to the special issue on trust in an organizational context." Organization Science **14**(1): 1.

Millen, D., R. and M. A. Fontaine (2003). Improving individual and organizational performance through communities of practice. Proceedings of the 2003 international ACM SIGGROUP conference on Supporting group work. Sanibel Island, Florida, USA, ACM.

Newell, S. and J. Swan (2000). "Trust and inter-organizational networking." Human Relations **53**(10): 1287-1328.

Nyhan, R. C. (2000). "Changing the Paradigm: Trust and its Role in Public Sector Organizations." The American Review of Public Administration **30**(1): 87-109.

Otis, B. (2007). Factors in Social Computing Related to Worker Productivity. Master of Science Capstone Report, University of Oregon.

Paino, M. and A. Rossett (2008). "Performance Support That Adds Value to Everyday Lives." Performance Improvement **47**(1): 37.

PaloAltoNetworks (2009). The Application Usage and Risk Report: An Analysis of End User Application Trends in the Enterprise. Sunnyvale, Palo Alto Networks: 1-19.

Perrow, C. (1967). "A Framework for the Comparative Analysis of Organizations." American Sociological Review **32**(2): 194-208.

Perry, R. (2006). Diffusion theories. Encyclopedia of Sociology. E. F. Borgatta and R. J. V. Montgomery. New York, Macmillan Reference USA, 2001. **1**: 674-681.

Porras, J. J., K. Hargis, K. J. Patterson, D. G. Maxfield, N. Roberts and R. J. Bies (1982). "Modeling-Based Organizational Development: A Longitudinal Assessment." Journal of Applied Behavioral Science **18**(4): 433-446.

Putnam, R. D. (1993). Bowling Alone. New York, Simon & Schuster Paperbacks.

Rhodes, J., P. Lok, R. Y.-Y. Hung and S.-C. Fang (2008). "An integrative model of organizational learning and social capital on effective knowledge transfer and perceived organizational performance." Journal of Workplace Learning 20(4): 245.

Rousseau, D. M., S. B. Sitkin, R. S. Burt and C. Camerer (1998). "Not so different after all: A cross-discipline view of trust." Academy of Management. The Academy of Management Review 23(3): 393.

Sabatini, F. (2009). "Social capital as social networks: A new framework for measurement and an empirical analysis of its determinants and consequences." Journal of Socio-Economics 38(3): 429-442.

Safko, L. (2012). The social media bible: tactics, tools, and strategies for business success. Hoboken, N.J, Wiley.

Sako, M. (1992). Prices, quality, and trust: inter-firm relations in Britain and Japan. Cambridge; New York, NY, USA, Cambridge University Press.

Segrest, S. L., D. J. Domke-Damonte, A. K. Miles and W. P. Anthony (1998). "Following the crowd: social influence and technology usage." Journal of Organizational Change Management 11(5): 425.

Shapiro, D. L., B. H. Sheppard and L. Cheraskin (1992). "Business on a handshake." Negotiation Journal 8: 365-377.

Shetzer, L. (1993). "A social information processing model of employee participation." Organization Science 4(2): 252.

Solis, B. and D. Breakenridge (2009). Putting the Public Back in Public Relations: How social media is reinventing the aging business of PR. Upper Saddle River, N.J., FT Press.

Vandermerwe, S. (1987). "Diffusing New Ideas In-House." The Journal of Product Innovation Management 4(4): 256.

Watson, D. L. and R. G. Tharp (1977). Self-directed behavior : self-modification for personal adjustment. Monterey, Calif., Brooks/Cole Pub. Co.

Williams, D. (2006). "On and Off the 'Net: Scales for Social Capital in an Online Era." Journal of Computer-Mediated Communication 11(2): 593-628.

Williamson, O. E. (1975). Markets and hierarchies: Analysis and anti-trust implications. New York, Free Press.

Williamson, O. E. (1985). The economic institutions of capitalism. New York, Free Press.

Withey, M., R. L. Daft and W. H. Cooper (1983). "Measures of Perrow's Work Unit Technology: An Empirical Assessment and a New Scale." The Academy of Management Journal 26(1): 45-63.

Wood, R. and A. Bandura (1989). "Social Cognitive Theory of Organizational Management." The Academy of Management Review 14(3): 361-384.

Woolcock, M. and D. Narayan (2000). "Social Capital: Implications for Development Theory, Research, and Policy." World Bank Res Obs 15(2): 225-249.

Zack, M. H. and J. L. McKenney (1995). "Social context and interaction in ongoing computer-supported management groups." <u>Organization Science</u> **6**(4): 394.

Zucker, L. G. (1986). Production of trust: Institutional sources of economic structure. <u>Research in organisational behaviour</u>. B. M. Staw and L. L. Cummings. Greenwich, CT, JAI. **8**.

Photo Credits

© Can Stock Photo Inc./Alexmit

© Can Stock Photo Inc./michaeldb

© Can Stock Photo Inc./LumaxArt2D

© Can Stock Photo Inc./niloo

© Can Stock Photo Inc./nmarques74

© Can Stock Photo Inc./michaeldb

© Can Stock Photo Inc./tashatuvango

© Can Stock Photo Inc./everythingpossible

© Can Stock Photo Inc./daisydaisy

© Can Stock Photo Inc./fotoscool

© Can Stock Photo Inc./thesupe87

© Can Stock Photo Inc./ijdema

Index

Y

About the Authors

Michael A. Brown, Sr., Ph.D.

Mike earned his Public Administration and Urban Policy degree, International Business, from Old Dominion University (ODU). He is teaching social media, public relations and crisis communication for three universities: Florida International University (FIU), ODU and University of Maryland University College (UMUC).

His online course at FIU, "Contemporary Issues in Public Administration (PAD5934), Social Media," was recognized by Quality Matters (QM) in 2013. QM is a nationally recognized faculty peer review for online and hybrid course design, signaling the best in education. http://www.qmprogram.org/qmresources/courses/index.cfm?year=2013&program=0.

He is currently the deputy director of Public Affairs for a joint military organization at Fort Eustis in Newport News, Va. Mike has 38 years of military and civilian experience and is a 24-year Air Force retiree.

Tracy Schario, APR

Tracy is a creative and responsive leader who enjoys working in fast-paced environments and leading cross-functional teams. At The Pew Charitable Trusts, she is the communications lead for its energy portfolio. Tracy teaches media relations at The George Washington University, and serves on the PRSA board of directors. She writes and speaks on media and PR strategy.

As spokesperson for The George Washington University, Tracy was frequently on television and managed several high profile crises receiving national media attention. She developed GW's social media plan and sustainability communications strategy, administered its award-winning news Web site and produced a weekly E-Newsletter.

Previously Tracy was vice president at a technology PR firm and worked for the U.S. Department of State in Indonesia and the Philippines where she received a Meritorious Honor award. Tracy earned her M.A. in communications from Ohio University and her B.A. from The Ohio State University.

Julie Ann Woodford Photography

Contact Us

DOC BROWN
dr.michael.brown76@gmail.com
LinkedIn: michaelbrown76
Mobile: (757) 876-6589
socialmedia4evr.com

TRACY SCHARIO, APR
LinkedIn: Tracy Schario
@TracySchario
schariojohnson.com